Moments in Time

Ojai Valley Inn and Spa

OJAI VALLEY INN & SPA

BY MARA PAPATHEODOROU

Moments in Time

Ojai Valley Inn and Spa

Copyright © 2013 by
Ojai Valley Inn and Spa
905 Country Club Road
Ojai, California 93023
Phone 855-697-8780
www.ojairesort.com

Cover Photography: Gaszton Gal
Writer: Mara Papatheodorou

Published by

An imprint of

A wholly owned subsidiary of Southwestern
P.O. Box 305142
Nashville, Tennessee 37230
1-800-358-0560

Editorial Director: Mary Cummings
Art Direction and Book Design: Starletta Polster
Project Manager: Julee Hicks

Library of Congress Control Number: 2013905688
ISBN: 978-0-87197-586-7

Manufactured in Canada
First Printing: 2013   5,000 copies

Moments in Time

Ojai Valley Inn and Spa

By Mara Papatheodorou

Table of Contents

Foreword

Lester and Renee Crown

Although our family is from Chicago, we consider the Ojai Valley Inn & Spa an extension of our home. We hope that all who visit feel the warmth and genuine friendliness that our staff has provided to so many over the past 90 years. We are very proud to be part of the Inn's history and hope that you will not only come away from your visit feeling rejuvenated and rested, but also as though you have found a home away from home.

Over the years we have expanded the Inn from its original 100 rooms to over 300 rooms. *The George Thomas/Billy Bell 18-hole Golf Course* has been returned to its original design through the work of Jay and Carter Morrish, and we have added new venues, including the 10,000-square-foot proprietor's home we call *Casa Elar*. With its proximity to Los Angeles, the Inn has always been a natural getaway for Hollywood's stars. Many of the great names from the past and now many of the current talents frequent the Inn, where they are able to unwind without distractions and be pampered as all guests of the Inn have come to expect.

From my father's first introduction to the Inn during the 1950s, to the family becoming 100% owner in the 1980s, the Inn has proven a tranquil retreat for not only our family but for all guests seeking to relax and enjoy the beautiful surroundings that are unique to the Ojai Valley. For almost 60 years now, and spanning five generations of Crown family members, the Ojai Valley Inn & Spa has been a special place for our family to visit and entertain. Director Frank Capra chose the Ojai Valley as the location for his Shangri-La when he filmed *Lost Horizon* in 1937. We agree wholeheartedly with his selection and have always felt that when one enters the valley, they have truly arrived in a magical place.

Please enjoy your stay.

Lester Crown

Lester Crown

Searching for Shangri La

Searching for the "Shangri Las" of this world—idyllic hideaways—have always been memorable adventures for me. And I've found them along the way. In fact, the joke in my family is that I was born clutching my passport. Lucky me to have parents who embraced the world's offerings and believed the best way to understand people and places was to go and to experience them. From there, my love of travel and appreciation of different cultures and cuisines grew. Wherever that took me, there was magic. I'm not talking about abracadabra kind of magic. I'm talking about those magical "Shangri La" moments that create one-of-a-kind memories.

Frank Capra got it right when he chose Ojai as the "Shangri La" location for his 1937 Oscar-winning classic *Lost Horizons*. That's what put this charming town on the map. The exquisite Topatopa Mountains and hearty oaks are alluring. The rich Chumash Indian heritage of the area and founder Edward Libbey's love of the land are evident everywhere. What I now understand is that the idyllic magic of Shangri La really does exist in beautiful Ojai, California, at the very special *Ojai Valley Inn and Spa*.

This book is a tribute to the Inn's ninetieth anniversary. The pages before you tell its incredible story, then and now. Writing this book to honor that milestone and this very unique venue has been a gift and a pleasure. The Inn's stunning setting, impressive history, and amazing amenities are all part of what makes it a remarkable soulful getaway. Each guest is encouraged to "find your moment," whatever that may be. I found mine, and I'll keep coming back for more. Find yours and enjoy your own version of Shangri La.

—Mara Papatheodorou

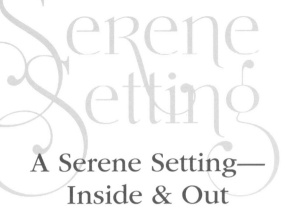

A Serene Setting—
Inside & Out

WHEN YOU FIRST ARRIVE AT THE INN, ITS SPANISH COLONIAL ARCHITECTURE AND THE BEAUTY OF ITS SETTING MAKE A WONDERFUL FIRST IMPRESSION. HOW THRILLING THAT WHAT YOU SEE ON THE OUTSIDE IS EXQUISITELY CARRIED THROUGH TO THE INSIDE OF YOUR ACCOMMODATIONS. EACH ONE OF THE 305 GUESTROOMS, WHICH INCLUDE THE SUITES AND PENTHOUSES, IS IMPECCABLY DESIGNED WITH THE UTMOST ATTENTION TO DÉCOR AND MODERN DETAILS. THE EXQUISITE DESIGN IS A PERFECT BLEND OF LUXURY AND STYLISH COMFORT.

"Spread your wings and escape from the

ordinary."

Inspired by the calming scent and hues of lavender, the Inn's signature botanical, subtle shades are woven throughout the newly refurbished look in the bedspreads, throw pillows, and carpets. These distinctive elements seamlessly bring the tranquility of the outdoor environs into each room. The refined rustic furniture—from desks and nightstands to chairs and wardrobes—is fashioned from distressed walnut and alder. Adding a subtle touch of Spanish influence, the worn, rough wood honors the past, while the technological upgrades such as iHome docking stations and HD TVs subliminally blend to meld the timeless legacy of the resort. Many rooms feature fireplaces, private balconies, or patios. And no matter what the room, each one has a view for you to enjoy, whether over a courtyard, the herb garden, the golf course, or the Topatopa mountain range.

Hacienda Suite

HACIENDA SUITE

Sumptuously appointed with an international look with Moroccan-inspired touches by well known architect Bill Mahan, this suite is the ultimate in luxury. Ideal for a honeymoon or corporate master suite, there are sweeping panoramic views of the Ojai Valley, a resplendent living room with fine imported European furniture, and a large fireplace. The dining room comfortably seats six and is well supported by a beautiful kitchenette to enhance any private eat-in entertaining.

Spa Suites

SPA SUITES

For the ultimate in privacy and luxury, the 1,500-square-foot penthouse suites offer an unmatched private spa experience in Southern California. These two-bedroom suites are located on the top floor of Spa Ojai and are accessed by a private key-controlled elevator in the Spa Village. Each beautifully appointed suite, whether the Sunrise or the Moonrise, features its own fireplace and full amenities with a balcony overlooking the spa pool and the beautiful Ojai Valley.

WALLACE NEFF ROOMS

Aptly named in honor of the original golf Clubhouse architect, Wallace Neff, these historical rooms offer the ambience and charm of a bygone era. Connected to the architectural award-winning Clubhouse, these twenty-two historical rooms were built in 1934 and offer a true sense of the place upon which the Inn was founded.

Family also includes four paws with a dog's wagging tail or a quiet kitty purr, and the Inn is proud to be a pet-friendly hotel. Service is strictly five-diamond and includes a gourmet pet menu, your pet's name on the outside of the room, and plenty of friendly areas to be walked.

CASA ELAR

Privacy extraordinaire is an ideal way to describe Casa Elar, the beautiful Italian-styled villa. This five-bedroom gated residence has a large motor court, two-car garage and even its own Bentley-inspired golf cart is a stately site. While there, you enjoy the comfort of this fully equipped 10,407-square-foot gorgeous home.

There are two master suites upstairs with spacious "his" and "her" bathrooms, two suites downstairs, outdoor balconies with fireplaces, a private spa and pool with a stunning view and shaded areas and a massage room with a fireplace and facilities for salon services. Cooking is a pleasure in the impressive gourmet kitchen or outside using the stone pizza oven and gas barbecue. Start with drinks in the library, which has an impressive built-in bar, and follow with lunch or dinner in the amazing dining room, which seats twelve, or on one of the lovely terraces overlooking the Valley.

But what's the best part of all? It is the best of both worlds—staying in the luxury of what feels like your own home with all the amenities of the Inn available and a private staff to take care of and meet any and every need and whim you desire.

19

Spirituality

Ojai and that Little Extra Something...

SPENDING TIME AT THE OJAI VALLEY INN IS A TRUE JOY AND A REAL PLEASURE. THE FANTASTIC ACTIVITIES, SPA, AND AMENITIES DO MAKE AN INCREDIBLE DIFFERENCE. BUT WHY IS IT SOME PLACES—LIKE THE INN AND ITS ENVIRONS—FEEL MORE SPECIAL AND DIFFERENT THAN OTHERS? AND WHAT IS "IT"—THAT LITTLE EXTRA SOMETHING— YOU JUST CAN'T PUT YOUR FINGER ON?

"Luxury that inspires,
that heals and comforts."

The "IT" Factor

Rest assured—there is an "IT" factor in the air and in the Valley that makes you breath deeper and your pulse slow down. The history of the area and its connection to the Chumash Indians is real. They had a rich heritage here with songs, dances, and legends and were physically and spiritually united with nature. The name *Ojai* translated from Chumash means "the moon." The tribe believed the location of the valley and the unique east-west position of its mountain ranges in relation to the moon was a sign of mystical powers, similar to those found in Sedona, Arizona, or Santa Fe, New Mexico. And so Ojai and the Valley has "IT"—that little extra something—that adds a powerful and pleasing natural aspect to the enjoyment of your memorable stay.

The Pink Moment

THERE IS SOMETHING SPECIAL ABOUT A STUNNING SUNSET THAT TAKES YOUR BREATH AWAY. AND OJAI DELIVERS THAT BRILLIANTLY WITH A MEMORABLE "PRETTY IN PINK" MOMENT AS THE SUN SETS. THE CITY'S UNIQUE LOCATION— 12 MILES INLAND FROM THE PACIFIC OCEAN— AND ITS TOPOGRAPHY—THE EAST-TO-WEST TOPATOPA MOUNTAIN RANGE—ALLOW THE FADING SUNLIGHT OF THE DAY TO CREATE A GLORIOUS SHADE OF PINK FOR SEVERAL MINUTES OVER BLUFFS THAT ARE 6,000 FEET ABOVE SEA LEVEL AT THE EAST END OF THE OJAI VALLEY.

There are places on the property where you can enjoy this magical colorful moment, from the golf course to the Maravilla veranda, while sipping one of the delicious pink cocktails or champagne which are the Inn's nod to this lovely phenomenon.

"Find your moment at the Ojai Valley Inn & Spa."

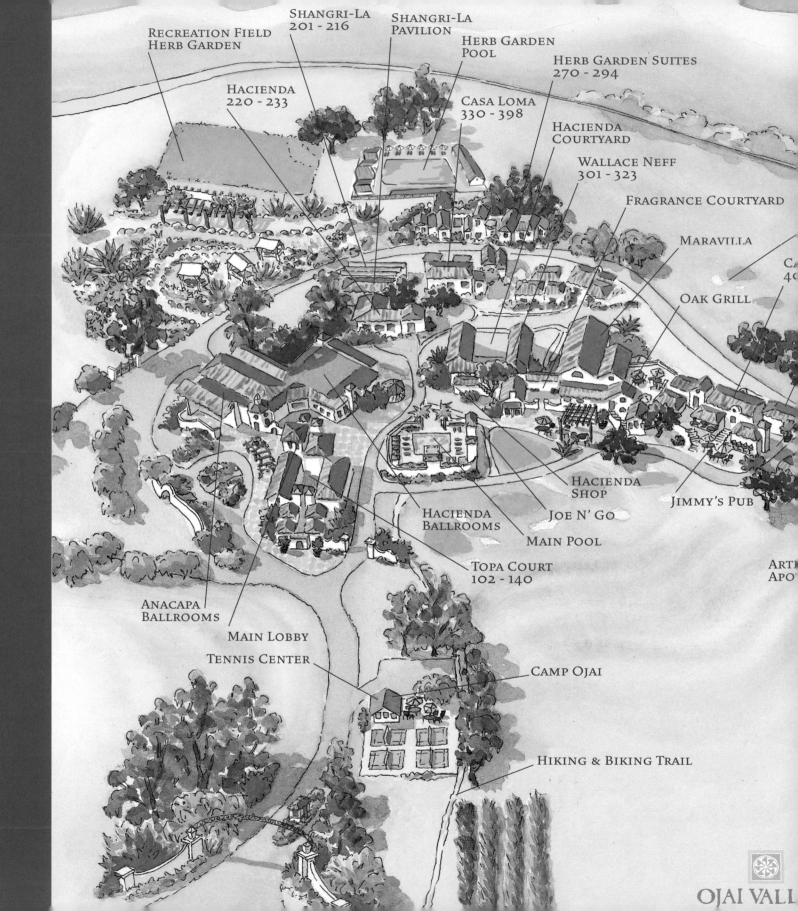

RECREATION FIELD
HERB GARDEN

HACIENDA
220 - 233

SHANGRI-LA
201 - 216

SHANGRI-LA
PAVILION

HERB GARDEN
POOL

CASA LOMA
330 - 398

HERB GARDEN SUITES
270 - 294

HACIENDA
COURTYARD

WALLACE NEFF
301 - 323

FRAGRANCE COURTYARD

MARAVILLA

OAK GRILL

HACIENDA
SHOP

JOE N' GO

JIMMY'S PUB

HACIENDA
BALLROOMS

MAIN POOL

TOPA COURT
102 - 140

ANACAPA
BALLROOMS

MAIN LOBBY

TENNIS CENTER

CAMP OJAI

ART...
APO...

HIKING & BIKING TRAIL

OJAI VALL

RANCH

RIVING RANGE

ROBLES
447

LOWER
PARKING LOT

GOLF SHOP

BIKE RENTAL

FONTANA
640 - 696

casa elar

ARBOLADA
601 - 631

CASA BLANCA
501 - 521

SPA & SPA BOUTIQUE
700 - 703

VILLA LOS PADRES
760 - 783

COTTAGE &
ECARY

VILLA MARIPOSA
704 - 723

PASEO VILLAS
730 - 751

M. Muns

INN & SPA

The Links

Ojai: One of the Best Golf Courses in the World

FOUNDER EDWARD LIBBEY HAD A DREAM TO CREATE A WORLD-CLASS GOLF COURSE AND COUNTRY CLUB AMIDST THE BEAUTY OF OJAI'S TOPATOPA MOUNTAINS THAT HE LOVED SO MUCH. HE HIRED RENOWNED DESIGNERS GEORGE C. THOMAS AND BILLY BELL WHO IN 1923 UNVEILED THEIR NEW GREEN GRASS CREATION. THEIR GOAL AND CHALLENGE WAS TO CREATE A GOLF COURSE WHERE THE AVERAGE GOLFER COULD ENJOY A ROUND WITHOUT TOO MUCH STRESS OR STRAIN AND WHERE THE ADVANCED PLAYER COULD BE TESTED TO SECURE PARS AND FINISH WITH A FINE SCORE. THEY SUCCEEDED ON EVERY LEVEL.

"A Shangri-La for golfers…"

Glorious Golf

Golfers then and now hail the Ojai Valley course as a glorious marvel of golfing ability and architecture.

During its ninety years, the golf course has given novices and experts alike great pleasure in play. The 18-hole, 70-par course and greens plays 6,292 yards and is considered one of the great golf resorts in the world. As a result, it has earned numerous accolades and a spot on the lists of specialty golf magazines and travel guides. It is especially revered for the way the course twists and turns to embrace the elements of the setting and the area's natural beauty of the Sycamore and eucalyptus trees.

The terrain has been made more famous by the pros and celebrities who have chosen it for exhibitions and competitions. Hollywood legends Bing Crosby and Bob Hope played here frequently in the '40s, '50s, and '60s, and current-day celebrities like Will Smith, Kevin Costner, and Michael Douglas (and his amazing golf-playing wife, Catherine Zeta-Jones) frequent the course. The romantic classic movie *Pat and Mike*, starring Katherine Hepburn and Spencer Tracy, a love story revolving around golf, was filmed here.

Golf legends Ben Hogan, Arnold Palmer, Sam Snead, Lee Trevino, and others have all played here. The Inn has also hosted seven Senior PGA events.

Legendary Golf Course

Legendary greats Ben Hogan, Sam Snead, Jack Nicklaus, and Lee Trevino have successfully tackled the course and celebrities such as Bing Crosby, Bob Hope, and Michael Douglas have all tried for a perfect scratch game. Each of the eighteen holes has a name highlighting its special significance or unique elements.

HOLE #1 (PLUM BLOSSOM)

The first hole is named after the plum trees located directly behind the first green that bloom a beautiful pink in the spring each year.

HOLE #2 (DEVIL'S CAULDRON)

This hole is named after the deep winding barranca that comes into play on the tee and approach shots to this hole. This hole was included in *Golf Magazine's* 500 Greatest Golf Holes.

HOLE #3 (SHORTY)

"Shorty" is the shortest golf hole design that George C. Thomas has implemented in any of his many golf courses.

HOLE #5 (CONDORS NEST)

This hole features an elevated tee shot into the valley below, and California Condors from the nearby Condor Sanctuary have been sighted overhead here.

HOLE #6 (MISTLETOE)

Abundant mistletoe growing in the sycamore trees along the left side of this hole gives it its name.

HOLE #7 (CROSBY'S CREEK)

Named after entertainer Bing Crosby who was an avid golfer and played here in the late '40s and early '50s, you have to carry Crosby's Creek on your approach shot to this green.

HOLE #4 (DEER CANYON)

Named after the deep canyon that you have to carry on your tee shot, this is the region of the course where you may spot a deer during your round of golf.

HOLE #8 (HOGAN'S HOLLOW)

This hole is named after golf legend Ben Hogan, who used to practice here during the West Coast swing of the PGA Tour with his fellow Texas Professional friend Jimmy Demaret.

HOLE #9 (EUCALYPTUS ALLEY)

This par five hole is lined on each side with five different types of eucalyptus trees (Tasmanian Gum, Blue Gum, Iron Bark, Globule, and White Box).

HOLE #10 (MATILIJA)

This hole is named after its perfect view of Matilaja Mountain and Canyon to the West.

HOLE #11 (PINK MOMENT)

This hole has a perfect view of the "Pink Moment." The "Pink Moment" happens right before sunset and paints the rock face of the Topatopa Mountains a beautiful pink color.

HOLE #12 (HONEYSUCKLE)

The finishing hole for all of the seven PGA Champions Tour events that were here from 1989–1996, this hole is named after the honeysuckle-covered fence that borders the golf course the entire length of this hole.

HOLE #13 (VALLEY OAK)

The large valley oak trees that overhang the tee and hotel pathway that is located nearby give this hole its name.

HOLE #15 (THE LANDING)

George Thomas landed his airplane near this hole when he was in the process of building the golf course.

HOLE #16 (CAPTAIN'S PRIDE)

This hole is named after Architect George Thomas, who was an avid yachtsman and nicknamed the "The Captain." It was featured in all of the three books written about him and his golf course architecture.

HOLE #17 (THE INSPIRATION)

This hole is named after the magnificent panoramic view of the Ojai Valley that you take in on the tee. Enjoy!

HOLE #14 (SANDER'S SNARE)

This hole is named after the flamboyant PGA Tour player Doug Sanders who represented the Ojai Valley Inn during the 1960s.

HOLE #18 (DEMARET'S CHALLENGE)

Named after PGA Tour player Jimmy Demaret, who represented the Ojai Valley Inn during the late 1940s and 1950s. Hole 18 is the most difficult hole on the golf course and a challenge for any level of golfer.

Spa Ojai Village

Embrace tranquility and calm when you enter the Spa Ojai Village courtyard. The babbling Moroccan tiled fountain, 50-foot belltower and inviting outdoor fireplace welcome you to the charm and ambience of this enchanting spa. Everything—from the various unique treatments, massages, and facials to sipping herbal tea or cucumber water on a chaise lounge while listening to soothing music—is here to enhance relaxation and encourage renewal. The 31,000-square-foot space, beautifully decorated with colorful tiles, includes two pools, a fully-equipped workout room, mind and body studio, and a boutique with clothes and amenities.

"A place for individuals..."

Your body and soul are nourished by any one of the special body remedies and wraps. The Shangri-La body treatment features a scrub made from local honey and lavender from the property, while the Kuyam experience highlights the Indian history of Ojai and combines the therapeutic effects of cleansing clay and essential oils. The spa also features fun sugar body polishes that change with the seasons: in winter, from December to February, a cocoa and pomegranate polish; in spring, from March to May, the Ojai Pixie tangerine polish; in summer, from June to August, lemon verbena and avocado; and in autumn, from September to November, pumpkin spice polish.

ESSENCE OF OJAI AMENITIES

A signature scent formulated at the Inn's Artist Cottage and Apothecary, the Essence of Ojai products—soap, shampoo, conditioner, and body lotion—are the guests' room amenities. Meticulously crafted from the herb garden's organic bounty, the calming qualities of lavender, the uplifting aroma of freshly picked citrus, and the grounding of wild and cultivated herbs are blended together to capture the region's energy and peacefulness. You can also purchase the products to take the essence of Ojai home. By using them, you can continue to awaken your senses and remind yourself of your blissful stay at the Inn.

The Artist Cottage

EXPLORE YOUR OWN ARTISTIC ABILITIES WHEN YOU VISIT THE INN'S VERY SPECIAL AND SERENE ARTIST COTTAGE. WHETHER YOU ARE A NOVICE OR AN EXPERT, THIS PEACEFUL, COMFORTABLE HAVEN ALLOWS YOU TO ENGAGE IN A PERSONAL JOURNEY OF DISCOVERY WITH YOURSELF, FRIENDS, OR FAMILY. YOU CAN BLEND COLOR POTIONS AND PAINT ON CANVAS, GLASS, SILK, OR TILES; CUT AND PASTE A COLLAGE, CREATE A PERSONAL MANDALA; OR SCRIBBLE AND DRAW. IN WHATEVER WAY YOU WANT TO BRING OUT THE INNER ARTIST IN YOU, THERE ARE GROUP-GUIDED ART ACTIVITIES OR PRIVATE SESSIONS WITH LOCALS FOR CHILDREN AND ADULTS.

An artist is an explorer. He must begin by self-discovery and the observation of his own procedures.

— Henri Matisse

THE APOTHECARY

The Inn embraces the fragrant elements and the natural herbs, flowers, and fruits of the area at its private Apothecary. A trained specialist mixes and matches oils to create your own fragrance. Aroma custom blending is an experience that will awaken your senses. This unique class helps you test and try different combinations to create your "just you" scent that can even become your own product line. There may be a touch of lavender, a drop of citrus, or a hint of mint in your personally designed elixir, perfume, or bath items. Part of the fun and intrigue is that you get to decide!

Ojai's Great Outdoors

As a guest at the Inn, there is plenty to do and many moments to enjoy. Play a round of golf or a game of tennis. Indulge in a spa treatment or relax by one of the pools. Take an art class or create your own scented oil at the apothecary. Meander the grounds on foot or by bicycle, linger in the herb garden, or read a book under one of the large Oaks.

"More than a place outside the city, a place inside of you..."

Splish, Splash!

Each of the four luxury pools at the resort offers a unique experience for guests to enjoy.

THE HERB GARDEN POOL

The setting of the Herb Garden Pool is serene and alluring. Nestled within the property's picturesque plantings of fruit trees, herbs, flowers, and vegetables, this adults-only pool is a wonderful place to sit and enjoy the peace and quiet of its surroundings. There is a hot tub with a grande fireplace, plush seating, and private cabana service. The Herb Garden Bistro serves innovative cocktails, appetizers, and sandwiches.

THE MAIN POOL

The Main Pool of the Inn is designed for all guests and is ideal for families. There is shaded and sunny placement of lounge chairs so everyone's preferences are accommodated. For a group of friends and relatives wanting more privacy to swim and lounge together, there are private cabanas available that include such extras as fresh fruit, bottled water, reading materials, and playing cards. The kiddie pool is fun for the little ones and the large hot tub is great for adults. The Swim Club Café features terrific items for breakfast, lunch, and snacks as well as delectable drinks and cocktails to enjoy at the café or poolside.

SPA LEISURE POOL & LAP POOL

Spa Ojai offers the ultimate in relaxation and rejuvenation, and the two pools in the Spa Village enhance the experience. The Spa Leisure Pool is enveloped by rose gardens and has a hot tub, luxurious seating, and beautiful views. Adjacent to that is the Lap Pool, which is sixty feet long and has a swim track for training and fitness along with a hot tub and a welcoming seating area. Café Verde is the spa restaurant, where health conscious cuisine for breakfast and lunch is available and freshly blended juices and smoothies are made to order.

If and when you do want to venture out into the town or around the vicinity to participate in other Ojai activities, the staff at the Inn knows just how to point you in the right direction.

LAKE CASITAS

The water jewel of the Ojai Valley is lovely Lake Casitas. For peace and quiet in a soothing setting on the water, experience world-class trophy bass fishing at the lake. There are high-performance rigged bass boats and deluxe pontoon boats available that will provide you with a fun and memorable day of fishing.

OJAI VINEYARD

For almost three decades, the Ojai Vineyard has been on the cutting edge of wine production in the Santa Barbara area. Founder and winemaker Adam Tolmach takes pride in crafting some of the most delicious, award-winning, and compelling wines on the Central Coast. Drop into the vineyard's downtown Tasting Room where you test and taste a flight of their wines to determine your favorites.

OJAI TROLLEY

The Ojai Trolley Service, reminiscent of a bygone era, has a stop at the Inn so guests can hop aboard to take a leisurely one-mile journey to the charming center of this historic town. Stroll down Main Street and weave in and out of art galleries, book stores, clothes shops, and diverse eateries.

Adventures

For a memorable outdoor adventure, without having to leave the Inn, take a geocache hike, which is a really fun and diverse way to enjoy the pathways and hidden havens around the 220-acre property. Led by a guide with GPS navigation in hand, curiosity-seekers embark on a picturesque hike with a treasure hunt premise that leads to all sorts of wonderful stories and surprises.

HORSEBACK RIDING

The Ojai Valley is home to many scenic trails, and taking a horseback ride along any of them showcases the beauty of the area in a unique way. Guests can wind through shady canyons and see the seasonal blooms, the towering Oaks, the Nordoff Ridge, and the spectacular views of the magnificent Topatopa Mountains. From beginners to advanced riders, no matter what your level or age, the different trail-riding companies accommodate you accordingly.

Casper & Friends

The setting of the Inn is an incredible sanctuary where you can unwind and replenish. It is also a sanctuary of sorts for some of the cutest feathery staff members on property—the menagerie of three parrots that meet, greet, and converse with visitors when they stroll or stop by the bird sanctuary.

Casper, an Australian Cockatoo who began calling the Inn his home in 2008, is the leader of the pack and proud to flaunt his snowy white crest and curved bill. He delights children and adults with his various swing tricks as well as his singing, barking, and laughing. Across the way, gal pal parrots Rudy, a beautiful red head, is happy to tell you her name and moo like a cow while Annie, an African grey, imitates sounds and whistles at guests.

Ojai's Festival Fun and Cultural Cache

With its pastoral landscapes and mountain ranges, its charming small town setting, artistic community, and the diversity of its activities, the Ojai Valley is truly a one-of-a-kind treasure that guests at the Inn enjoy. Every year locals and visitors come to this artisan community to attend the different unique festivals and tournaments that the people of Ojai host. Hence a reason why Ojai is considered California's Shangri-La!

OJAI TENNIS TOURNAMENT

Referred to as "The Ojai" by locals and players alike, this is California's oldest and largest amateur tennis tournament. Started in 1896 by William Thacher, this April event is now a rite of passage for any serious young tennis player looking to break onto the circuit. More than just a tournament,

OJAI WINE FESTIVAL

From its humble beginnings in 1987, the Ojai Wine Festival, sponsored by the Rotary Club, has become a leading regional June event. Wine and beer connoisseurs delight in tasting reds, whites, and rosés from over sixty of California's award-winning wineries and fifteen excellent premium beers and microbrews. Local restaurants serve delicious food, artists and galleries display their works, musicians entertain, and free boat rides on beautiful Lake Casitas complete a memorable afternoon.

it truly is an Ojai tradition. Many tennis greats have played here, including Arthur Ashe, Billie Jean King, Stan Smith, Jimmy Connors, Tracy Austin, Michael Chang, Lindsay Davenport, and Pete Sampras. There is an entire list of Ojai Wall of Fame members on the plaques at the tennis grandstands at Libbey Park.

OJAI LAVENDAR FESTIVAL

The Ojai Lavendar Festival obviously celebrates everything lavender. The Valley's Mediterranean climate makes it ideal growing ground for this colorful crop. Growers and producers created this fun and fragrant late June festival, and they are proud to promote and share their knowledge and products. Locals and visitors alike come to Libbey Park to marvel at the sights and soothing aromas of its many varieties and textures. From the expected to the unexpected, smell it, wear it, taste it. Enjoy lavender in all sorts of ways!!

OJAI MUSIC FESTIVAL

From its founding in 1947, the Ojai Music Festival has created a place for groundbreaking musical experiences by bringing together innovative artists and curious audiences within the intimate set-up of Libbey Bowl. The four-day June festival attracts some of the world's greatest musicians and features concerts, symposiums, films, and

become a prominent event for industry professionals and yet-to-be-discovered aspiring filmmakers. Started in 1999, the October festival features an eclectic and exciting range of unsung heroes in the business. The screening of films and panel discussions create an intimate atmosphere that is in line with the low-key yet sophisticated tone of the town. In many ways, Ojai becomes as much a star of the event as the festival winners themselves.

OJAI DAY

Ojai Day, celebrated on the third Saturday of every October, is the most popular festive event of the year. Similar to a street fair, it is as unique as the city itself. The rich artistic, agricultural, and cultural heritage of the Valley is highlighted by the participation of local artisans, musicians, and vendors, including the Ojai Valley Inn & Spa, of course! Ojai Day was originally created by residents in the early 1920s to thank glass magnate Edward Libbey for his generous donations that funded the building of the downtown Arcade and the post office with its sixty-five–foot tall belltower.

community events. Considered a highlight of the summer season, Ojai remains a leader in the classical music arena, reinforcing why music matters.

OJAI FILM FESTIVAL

Just ninety miles from Los Angeles, considered the film capital of the world, the Ojai Film Festival has

Celebrations that Become Memories

Celebrations of every kind are about finding moments that become memories together. They are a time to pause, to enjoy, to live, to love, and to laugh with family, friends, and one another. And there is no better place to share your memorable event together than at the Inn. The breathtaking setting of the southern California mountains and the tranquility of the Ojai Valley create a majestic atmosphere for your special day that will leave a lasting impression.

"*Memories in the making...*"

Weddings

Marriage is a symbol of a new beginning of your journey together. The resort features several stunning wedding venues—from the intimate to the dramatic—that make your ceremony and reception a time to remember and a dream come true.

A great scene can be set for other types of gatherings, too, whether big or small, from reunions to birthday parties or business meetings. It's all here to create your moments and memories.

"Take the path less traveled."

Ojai Valley Inn & Spa
1923–2013

Ninety Years Young and Strong!

THROUGHOUT THE YEARS, HOSTING MANY CELEBRITIES, MUSICIANS, DIGNITARIES, AND POLITICIANS, OJAI VALLEY INN & SPA RETAINS ITS SENSE OF PLACE, STAYING TRUE TO THE PEOPLE WHO FIRST BUILT IT. AMID AN UNSURPASSED NATURAL LANDSCAPE WITH DIVERSE APPEAL TO FAMILIES, COUPLES, GOLFERS, AND MULTIGENERATIONAL GUESTS, THE INN REMAINS ONE OF THE FINEST RESORTS IN NORTH AMERICA AND IS A MEMBER OF THE PREFERRED HOTEL GROUP AND THE HISTORIC HOTELS OF AMERICA.

90th 1923-2013
OJAI VALLEY
INN & SPA
Celebrating 90 Legendary Years

1923–2013

OJAI VALLEY INN AND SPA
NINETY YEARS YOUNG AND STRONG!

1916 — Mr. Libbey starts acquiring land in the valley. The town of Nordhoff is renamed Ojai, the Chumash Indian name for "moon."

1900s	**1910s**

1908 — Edward D. Libbey, a prosperous glass manufacturer, vacations in Nordhoff (Ojai) and the valley.

1917 — Most of the town is destroyed in a fire. Mr. Libbey helps create what has become today's downtown Ojai.

90th **1923-2013**
OJAI VALLEY
INN & SPA
Celebrating 90 Legendary Years

1934 — Architect Austin Pierpont constructs a tiled hallway and twenty-two guest rooms per the original drawings of Wallace Neff, connecting the guestrooms and the clubhouse. These rooms are now known as the Wallace Neff Historical Rooms.

1942 — A different kind of glory distinguishes the Ojai Valley Country Club as it is transformed during World War II into Camp Oak, a military training center for a battalion of 1,000 Army troops.

1930s	**1940s**

1937 — Director Frank Capra depicts the Valley's panoramic mountain vistas as the mythical Shangri-La for his film, *Lost Horizon*. The release of the movie brings Hollywood stars to the hideaway resort, where year-round sunny climate and golf rounds played amid breathtaking scenery are enjoyed daily. Today the Valley retains the allure of the Shangri-La image.

1925 — Mr. Libbey dies of pneumonia. Sadly, he never sees his hotel built; however, the architectural plans were safely archived.

1920s

1923 — Millionaire glass manufacturer Edward D. Libbey purchases 220 acres of Ojai land to pursue his dream of building a private country club and golf course that will harmonize with the unspoiled beauty of his favorite rural paradise. When finished, he enjoys playing on his new golf course and visiting the clubhouse, designed by renowned architect Wallace Neff.

Ojai Valley Inn and Country Club *golf scorecard*

1944 — The Army turns the base over to the United States Navy for a rest and recuperation facility. When the government finally auctions off the last of the Quonset huts and barracks, the property is returned to private ownership.

1947 — The resort reopens as *Ojai Valley Inn and Country Club*. The Glamour Era of the Inn begins. It becomes known as the hideaway resort for Hollywood's brightest stars seeking the tranquil pleasures of the valley.

1946 — Wealthy investor Don Burger, along with influential investors including Irene Dunne, Loretta Young, and Tom Lewis, purchases the property.

1923–2013

OJAI VALLEY INN AND SPA
NINETY YEARS YOUNG AND STRONG!

1950s   **1960s**

1952 — The movie *Pat and Mike*, starring Katherine Hepburn and Spencer Tracy, is filmed at the Inn.

Late 1950s to 1980s — The 1st American Volunteer Group, a group composed of U.S. pilots from the Army, Navy, and Marine Corps and famously nicknamed the "Flying Tigers," hold their annual reunions at the Inn every other year during Fourth of July weekend.

1987 — Golf course architect Jay Moorish is commissioned to renovate the golf course.

'80s to '90s
Seven Senior PGA Tournaments are held at the Inn.

1980s   **1990s**

1985 — The Crown family of Chicago purchases the property. They instill a $50 million dollar renovation where they add a new lobby, 218 guest rooms, and a new conference center. The Crown family remains the Inn's owner today.

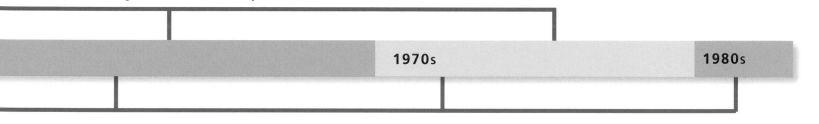

Late 1950s, '60s and '70s — The Glamour Years are thriving and in full swing, where Hollywood notables visit frequently and enjoy lavish parties. Celebrities such as Clark Gable, Anthony Quinn, Imogene Coca, Joan Crawford, George Gobel, and Jane Wyman visit often. Movies and TV shows are filmed at the Inn.

1970s   **1980s**

1990   Jack Nicholson and Harvey Keitel, *The Two Jakes*

1991 — The Inn joins the Historic Inns of America

1997 — *Benchmark Spa Ojai* is completed under the direction of architect Bill Mahan. The resort becomes known as Ojai Valley Inn & Spa.

1923–2013

OJAI VALLEY INN AND SPA
NINETY YEARS YOUNG AND STRONG!

2003 — A $90 million property-wide renovation begins.

2000s

2000 — The 100th anniversary of the famed *Ojai Tennis Tournament* is celebrated, with some matches being played at the Inn.

2002 — Michael Douglas Golf Tournament

2006 — The Artist Cottage and Apothecary opens.

2006 — The resort wins its first coveted AAA Five Diamond Award for excellence in the hospitality industry. It has achieved this distinguished accolade annually since 2006.

2005 — The major renovation of the Inn is completed. While preserving its original charming architecture and unique sense of place, the resort debuts 308 guest rooms and suites, a new lobby and entrance, new golf shop, new restaurants, new ballrooms, and meeting spaces.

OJAI VALLEY INN & SPA

2012 — The Inn wins the prestigious Condé Nast Traveler's Readers Choice Award.

2010s

2013 — The Ojai Valley Inn & Spa celebrates its ninetieth anniversary—ninety years young! A $5.5 million refurbishment renovation is finished.

Aerial view of Ojai Country Club.

(left) Portrait of Edward Libbey. (bkgd.) Putting the finishing touches on the Ojai Arcade in late 1916.

"He contributed freely to such institutions as were for the general good, his action springing from a heart filled with love and good feeling for humanity." –Sheridan

EDWARD LIBBEY

Edward Drummond Libbey (1854-1925), a wealthy glass manufacturer and philanthropist from Ohio, is largely credited with bringing about a major renaissance to Ojai's downtown area. While spending a winter in Ojai at the new Foothills Hotel in 1908, Libbey became captivated by the area's charm and beauty. In 1910, he built his first home on Fairview Road, and two years later purchased a ranch. In 1916, he commissioned San Diego architect Richard Requa to build a downtown arcade and post office with its signature tower. After two fires devastated the town in 1917, Libbey quickly became involved in helping the area recover, investing in the El Roblar Hotel and helping to fund a million gallon reservoir. Libbey donated seven acres in the center of the village and in 1917 presented it to the town for a community park. He then commissioned San Diego architect Richard Requa to build a downtown arcade and post office with its signature tower. In 1921, he set his sights on building a golf course, and two years later purchased 200 acres that had once been part of the Dunn ranch at a cost of $200,000 and built Ojai Country Club. Libbey hoped to add a hotel to the property, but he died on November 13, 1925 and was never able to enjoy his masterpiece. His plans, drawn by architect Wallace Neff, inspired the work of later architects who designed the renovation of the resort in 2004.

OJAI VALLEY INN & SPA

TO EDWARD DRUMMOND LIBBEY:
WE DEDICATE THIS YEARBOOK

"A man whose practical idealism, Whose love of the beautiful, Whose vision of altruistic service, Has inspired and brought to pass A great work in the Ojai Valley – All esthetic endowment of such Wondrous value That no man can contemplate it Without Spiritual uplift."

— Nordhoff students from the class of 1917 printed this tribute in their yearbook, the Topatopa Annual

The Libbey Connection

EDWARD DRUMMOND LIBBEY, A PROSPEROUS GLASS MANUFACTURER, FIRST CAME TO OJAI FOR A VACATION IN THE WINTER OF 1908 TO ESCAPE THE COLD OF TOLEDO, OHIO. THE VALLEY'S ROLLING HILLS AND TOPATOPA MOUNTAINS ENTHRALLED HIM. THE RAMSHACKLE RUSTIC WESTERN TOWN, THEN CALLED NORDHOFF, DID NOT. BUT MR. LIBBEY WAS A VISIONARY AND PHILANTHROPIST. HE SAW THE AREA'S POTENTIAL AND BELIEVED THE BREATHTAKING SURROUNDINGS COULD BE COMPLEMENTED BY A BEAUTIFUL YET-TO-BE DESIGNED TOWN CENTER.

In 1916, Edward Libbey began to acquire land in the valley and worked with prominent residents to bring his plan to fruition. Around the same time, citizens had also decided to acknowledge the area's Chumash Indian heritage by renaming the town Ojai, the

Chumash word for "moon." An unexpected fire in 1917 destroyed most of the town, leaving it in need of rescue and repair. With his vision, money, and contacts, Libbey intervened and helped create what has become today's downtown Ojai.

He built the Spanish-style arcade on Main Street and the post office and belltower that still stand. They are now the iconic symbols of the village. The pergola opposite the arcade was destroyed in an explosion in 1971, but it was rebuilt in 2000 to complete the Colonial architectural look.

Downtown Ojai, 1943

...ard Drummond Libbey
...to you and the members
...ly the courtesies
...f the
...Country Club
...California
...arch 20th 1921?

...will make it convenient to accept th...
...st and most picturesque golf cour...
...Mr. Geo. C. Thomas, Jr, and construct...

...eady for play, eighteen playable ab...
...eady for service.

Ojai Day was created in 1917 as a thank-you to Mr. Libbey, who disapproved of calling it Libbey Day but was excited that citizens appreciated all the new town had become. Libbey Park and Libbey Bowl are two venues named to honor him and to remind us of his everlasting contribution and legacy.

In 1923 Libbey's love of golf led him to develop the Ojai Valley Inn Golf Course and Country Clubhouse with the help of outstanding architect Walter Neff. He was delighted that the result highlighted the natural terrain of the mountains and the valley so well. He had plans designed, too, for the building of the Inn that came to be. But sadly, his untimely death in 1925 prevented him from seeing it completed. Yet somehow one knows he would be thrilled that when today's guests come to the Inn, they are as enthralled by the magic of Ojai as he was when he first visited in 1908.

"Find your own glamorous moments!"

Eternally Glamorous

IT WAS LEGENDARY DIRECTOR FRANK CAPRA WHO FIRST SHARED THE MAGICAL SPELL OF OJAI WITH MOVIEGOERS AND REAL HOLLYWOOD STARS. HIS 1937 OSCAR-WINNING CLASSIC *LOST HORIZONS* HIGHLIGHTED IDYLLIC SHANGRI-LA— WHICH WAS IN TRUTH OJAI, WHERE THE MOVIE WAS FILMED. THE IMPRESSION WAS SUCH THAT OJAI IS STILL CALLED CALIFORNIA'S SHANGRI-LA. THE INN, WITH ITS SETTING AND STYLE, FOLLOWS SUIT PERFECTLY.

From the glamour and glitz of '40s and '50s Old Hollywood to the current casual chic New Hollywood, those in the public eye, then and now, retreat at the Inn for fun, rest, and relaxation. The list is long and impressive, from Irene Dunne, Loretta Young, Judy Garland, and Jayne Mansfield enjoying themselves to Clark Gable, Bing Crosby, Bob Hope, and Buddy Hackett playing the golf course. Fred MacMurray got married here, and real-life lovebirds Spencer Tracy and Katharine Hepburn adored the Inn while playing golfers in their 1952 comedy *Pat and Mike*. In more recent years, Renee Zellweger, *Twilight* stars Kristen Stewart and Robert Pattinson, Toby Maguire, Michael Douglas and Catherine Zeta-Jones, and Will Smith and Jada Pinkett Smith have all been guests.

"There's really just one important difference between Shangri-La and Ojai. Shangri-La doesn't exist."

–E. Michael Johnson

The community known as Ojai was originally settled by the Oak Grove People more than eight thousand years ago. The Chumash Indians arrived around 1,000 B.C. and named it "Aw'ha'y," often translated as "the nest" or "the moon." When the Spanish and mission societies inhabited the area in the eighteenth century, they adopted the name Ojai. In 1874, R. G. Surdam purchased 1,606 acres of land and planned a town site. The town was first named Nordhoff in 1884 in honor of *New York Herald* correspondent Charles Nordhoff, who had written so glowingly about the area that many wealthy Easterners established winter residences here. The charming little town nestled in the valley surrounded by the Topa Topa mountains grew rapidly. The community's first newspaper, named *The Ojai*, was published in 1891. Twenty-six years later, in 1917, the residents officially changed the town name to Ojai. Known for its clean air, serene atmosphere and healthy lifestyle, Ojai soon became a well-known resort community. Brochures promoting tourism during that time promised visitors: "You sense the calm, the strange spirit of time and solitude which hovers about the Valley—eternal, unforgettable, and indescribable—truly a Valley of Enchantment."

L-R: Mrs. Ray Milland, Tom Lewis, Irene Dunne, Henry Luce, Loretta Young, New Year's Eve 1947 at Ojai Valley Inn and Country Club

Irene Dunne, late 1940s

Fred MacMurray and June Haver, early 1950s

Spencer Tracy and Katharine Hepburn, 1950s in Pat and Mike, *filmed at Ojai Valley Inn and Country Club.*

Mr. and Mrs. Jim Backus, New Year's Eve at Ojai Valley Inn and Country Club, circa 1953

Throughout its history, from yesteryears to today, the Inn has had and maintains an alluring appeal for the celebrity circuit and even for U.S. presidents (both President Carter and President Reagan visited the Inn.) No matter how you define it or whose visit defines it, no matter when or what the decade, there has always been something glamorous about the place. Perhaps it's the understated elegance of its décor, the discreet and loyal staff and service or its nestled, picturesque location that creates the attraction—you decide. Find your own glamorous moments!

HOLLYWOOD COMES TO OJAI

Ojai has always been a popular destination for Hollywood stars and directors. In 1937, Frank Capra used the sweeping mountain vistas as the backdrop for the mythical Shangri-La in his film *Lost Horizon*. In 1952, George Cukor selected Ojai for his film *Pat and Mike*, starring Katharine Hepburn and Spencer Tracy. In the 1970s, Ojai was the fictional home of Lindsey Wagner who starred in the popular television series, *The Bionic Woman*. Jack Nicholson filmed *The Two Jakes*, the sequel to *Chinatown*, at the resort in 1990. Dozens of Hollywood stars have stayed at Ojai over the years, including Judy Garland, Clark Gable, Walt Disney, Irene Dunne, Jane Wyman and Jimmy Stewart, Rory Calhoun and his wife Lita Baron, and Loretta Young and Tom Lewis honeymooned at Ojai. Rita Hayworth, Lana Turner and Joe DiMaggio often stayed at the Inn to visit their children who were attending local private schools. Raymond Massey and his family visited every Christmas. Nancy and Ronald Reagan were frequent visitors. Fred McMurray and June Haver were married in 1954 in a cottage on the fairway. Today, a new generation of stars continues to enjoy the beauty and privacy that the Inn has always promised.

OJAI VALLEY INN & SPA

James Stewart

Ronald and Nancy Reagan at Ojai Valley Inn and Country Club

Jack Nicholson, filming The Two Jakes

June Allison and Dick Powell, early 1950s

Jane Powell and Patrick Nerney wedding, 1954

Flying Tigers at the Inn

One of the Inn's most noted associations has been with the famed Flying Tigers, officially known as the 1st American Volunteer Group. From the 1950s through the 1980s, every other Fourth of July these heroes would reunite for a weekend of golf, relaxation, and wartime reminiscing. They were an air unit of pilots from the U.S. Army, Navy, and Marine Corps who were recruited under the secret authority of President Franklin D. Roosevelt to augment China's Air Force fighting against the Japanese.

From December 1941 to July 1942, these brave men used their piloting prowess to "fly like tigers" and succeeded in their missions. Years later these patriots believed the Inn's involvement as a combat training base in World War II and their special history made it the perfect place to hold a reunion and celebrate their camaraderie.

FLYING TIGERS RETURN TO OJAI

For over forty years, members of the historic Flying Tigers held their reunion here at the Inn. Three of their legendary members recently returned at the request of Ojai's Military Gallery to autograph a special edition of one thousand color lithographs of the P-40 fighter they made famous during their daring missions over the "Burma Hump" in the early days of WW II.

Pictured are Flying Tigers Hon. Charles H. Older, Tex Hill and president Dick Rossi. The litho is available for purchase at the Military Gallery - phone (805) 640-0057

From dinner menus to catering to room selection, I look forward to coordinating everything and being on-call when any of my groups visit.

"Although small professional and business groups instantly recognize the benefits of such on-property service, I also want to encourage social groups to avail themselves," Honea stresses. "Since the Inn is such a perfect place to get together with friends or relatives for golf, tennis, hiking, mountain biking or horseback riding, to hold a family reunion, to celebrate a birthday or anniversary or simply to meet for a respite, we want to make a social group's stay as rewarding as our professional/business guests' experience."

Honea's services are available by contacting your travel advisor or calling the Inn's sales department toll-free at (800) 422-OJAI (6524).

AMERICAN VOLUNTEER GROUP
A NATIONAL AVIATION CORPORATION
ALLEY INN • OJAI, CALIFORNIA
JULY 3-4-5, 1969

Jane Mansfield and friends, 1944

77

Entertainment

BOB HOPE AND BING CROSBY

Bob Hope and Bing Crosby entertain the troops with Exhibition Golf. During the early 1940s, the military used Ojai Valley Country Club's grounds for training facilities. The grounds were later used for rest and recuperation.

Ojai Valley Inn Golf Clubhouse

George C. Thomas, Jr., golf course architect

WORLD WAR II AND THE LOST HOLES

Just what is the story of World War II and the Lost Holes of Ojai? In 1942, as American involvement in World War II escalated, The Libbey Foundation leased the course and club to the U.S. Army for use as a combat training base. The first contingent to arrive was the 134th Nebraska Infantry. The Navy maintained a presence of practice there for the balance of the war until it ended in August of 1945.

As a result, two of the original holes—Holes 7 and 8—as designed by George Thomas and Billy Bell in 1923 were "lost" in weeds and overgrowth from its military use and then overlooked through the years of course makeovers. Rediscovered old photos indicated the course wasn't exactly as it was when it began. In the end, perseverance by and the curiosity of the Inn's pros paid off. In 1999, nearly 80 years after they were designed and 58 years after they disappeared during WWII, these 2 Thomas-designed holes were restored within their original layout and reintroduced by the Inn's pros. Now these holes remain two of the most beautiful and challenging ones on the course.

The Ojai Valley Inn golf course houses U.S Army troops, 1942–1945

LOCAL RULES
The rules of the USGA apply except as modified by the following local rules:

1. **HAZARDS**
All barrancas are water hazards. Lateral hazards are defined by red stakes and transverse hazards by white stakes. Ball played into a lateral water hazard may be dropped out 2 club lengths on either side with penalty of one stroke; see USGA Rule 33 (3b).

2. **OBSTRUCTIONS**
The following shall be treated as immovable obstructions (drop away 2 club lengths without penalty; see USGA Rule 31 (2)).
   (a) All cart paths, black top roads and roads traversing the fairways at approximately a right angle.
   (b) The drainage ditch on No. 14, No. 15 & road on No. 14.
   (c) Earth cracks;
   (d) Tree basins and staked trees;
   (e) All cart restraining ropes.

Ojai Valley Inn and COUNTRY CLUB
Please REPLACE ALL DIVOTS and REPAIR BALL BRUISES.

Ojai Valley Inn
and Country Club
Ojai, California

"Where Golf and the Weather get Together."

Ojai Valley Inn Country Club entrance, 1955

George Gobel and Bill Briggs, 1956

Jack Carson, Bill Briggs, Frankie Laine, Celebrity Ojai
Valley Inn, July 1956

Golf carts, 1960s

Martha Tilton and Bill Briggs, 1965

Mr. and Mrs. George Gobel and guest

Bill Briggs, Jo Stafford, Paul Weston, 1965

Jimmy Demaret

JIMMY DEMARET, OJAI'S MOST FAMOUS TOURING GOLF PROFESSIONAL, IS A LEGEND UNTO HIMSELF AND WITHIN THE COMMUNITY. WHEN YOU ARE PLAYING THE COURSE AND EVENTUALLY MAKE IT TO HOLE #18, *DEMARET'S CHALLENGE*, YOU'LL EITHER CURSE HIM OR THANK HIM SINCE IT'S CONSIDERED THE MOST CHALLENGING HOLE OF ALL, NO MATTER WHAT YOUR LEVEL! DEMARET WAS THE INN'S TOURING PROFESSIONAL FROM 1947 TO 1951 DURING WHICH TIME HE BROUGHT WORLDWIDE ATTENTION TO THE EXCELLENT COURSE AND INTRODUCED THE GREENS TO MANY OF HIS CRONIES WHO WERE CHAMPIONS AND PROFESSIONALS IN THEIR OWN RIGHT.

Over a thirty year golfing career, Demaret won thirty-one PGA tournaments from 1935 to 1957 and was the first golfer to win the Masters three times. He was also on three Ryder Cup teams and holds a six win, no loss record for those tournaments. On the circuit, he was known for his wit and humor and his colorful attire that earned him the fan nickname "The Wardrobe."

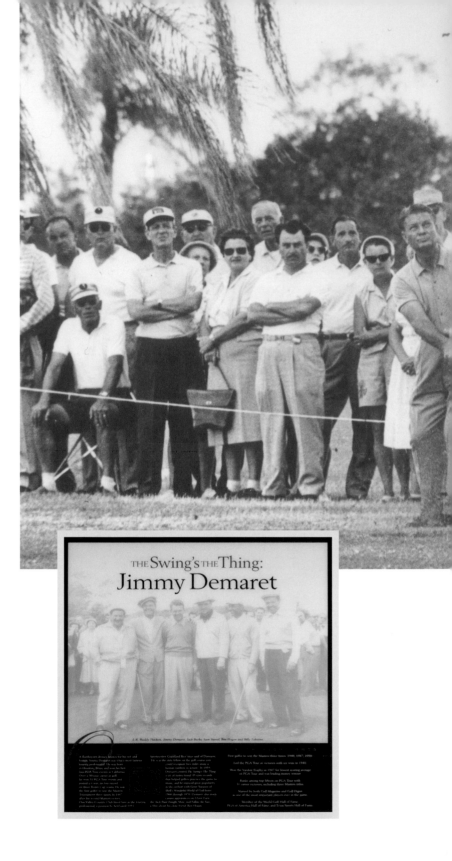

With his outgoing personality, Demaret dabbled in television where he even played a cameo of himself on the *I Love Lucy* show in 1954. He went on to become one of first golf professionals to become involved in broadcasting when he co-hosted *Shell's Wonderful World of Golf* from 1968 to 1970.

He was elected to the *World Golf Hall of Fame* in 1983 and has been ranked as the 20th greatest golfer of all time by *Golf Digest Magazine*.

But perhaps his happiest honor of all would be the Inn's tribute to him, *Jimmy's Pub* which serves great post-game drinks and delicious casual fare for lunch and dinner.

HOLE #18 (DEMARET'S CHALLENGE)

Named after PGA Tour player Jimmy Demaret who represented the Ojai Valley Inn during the late 1940s and 1950s, Hole 18 is the most difficult hole on the golf course and a challenge for any level of golfer.

Ben Hogan

BEN HOGAN, AN AMERICAN GOLFING LEGEND, IS CONSIDERED ONE OF THE GREATEST PLAYERS IN THE HISTORY OF THE GAME. WHEN YOU ARE PLAYING THE COURSE, CHECK OUT HOLE #8, *HOGAN'S HOLLOW*—A TRIBUTE TO HIM AS WELL AS ONE OF THE INN'S RESTORED LOST HOLES. GOOD BUDDY AND FELLOW TEXAN JIMMY DEMARET WAS THE TOURING PROFESSIONAL FOR THE INN'S GOLF COURSE AND CLUB, SO HE AND BEN PLAYED THE COURSE PROFESSIONALLY AND SOCIALLY THROUGHOUT THE '40S AND '50S. HOGAN PRACTICED HERE DURING THE WEST COAST PART OF THE PGA TOUR AND LIKED THE IMPRESSIVE TERRAIN.

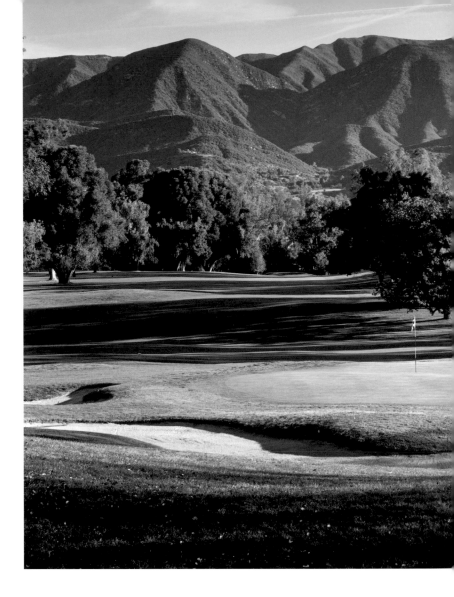

Hogan is noted for his profound influence on the golf swing theory and his renowned ball-striking ability. Nicknamed "*The Hawk*" because of his fierce determination and iron will, he was an intimidating opponent in tournaments. This served him well, as his nine career major championships place him fourth behind Jack

Nicklaus, Tiger Woods, and Walter Hagen. He is still only one of five professionals to have won all four major championships open to professionals (the Masters, the British Open, the U.S. Open, and the PGA Championships.) He was elected into the World Golf Hall of Fame in 1974.

Hogan developed a "secret" swing that always worked for him. He attributed it to a special wrist movement called "cupping under." He went on to write *Five Lessons: The Modern Fundamentals of Golf,* which remains one of the best books written about how to play.

HOLE #8 (HOGAN'S HOLLOW)

This hole is named after golf legend Ben Hogan, who used to practice here during the West Coast swing of the PGA Tour with his fellow Texas Professional and friend Jimmy Demaret.

Golf Greats

Arnold Palmer, 1970s

Arnold Palmer, Jimmy George

Golf Pro, Doug Sanders teeing off, 1970s

Golfers through the oak tree, 1970s

Dignitaries

1990 UNITED STATES-JAPANESE SUMMIT

OJAI VALLEY INN WAS THE SITE FOR THE INAUGURAL CLOSED-DOOR CONFERENCE OF THE UNITED STATES-JAPANESE SUMMIT IN 1990. FORMER JAPANESE PRIME MINISTER, YASUHIRO NAKASONE, ALONG WITH THIRTY OTHER POLITICAL AND BUSINESS DIGNITARIES, INCLUDING FORMER PRESIDENTS GERALD FORD AND JIMMY CARTER, WERE IN ATTENDANCE.

Mrs. Roosevelt Declares Americans Must Live as World Leaders

Mrs. Eleanor Roosevelt, guest of honor at a tea held at Ojai Valley Inn and Country Club, 1954

Spring

Summer

Autumn

Winter

Tastes for All Seasons

MEMORABLE MOMENTS AND MEALS ARE CERTAINLY A DELICIOUS PART OF YOUR EXPERIENCE AT THE INN. CALIFORNIA'S CENTRAL COAST IS CELEBRATED FOR THE WAYS ITS MEDITERRANEAN MICROCLIMATE COAXES THE WORLD'S BEST SEASONAL FOODS FROM ITS FERTILE ORCHARDS, RANCHES, FARMS, OCEAN WATERS, AND VINEYARDS. THIS IS CALIFORNIA COASTAL CUISINE AT ITS BEST AND MOST FRESH. IN SPRING, SUMMER, AUTUMN, AND WINTER, THE TEAM OF CHEFS AT THE INN MAKES THE MOST OF THE YEAR-ROUND BOUNTIES TO CREATE DELECTABLE SIGNATURE CUISINE.

Each culinary destination's menu uses fresh, sustainable ingredients. Within the 200-acre grounds, organic produce is grown, and the landscaping team uses all-natural, 100% organic methods in the tomato and herb gardens where rosemary, sage, thyme, tarragon, and lavender flourish. Fruit trees abound in the orchard, which features Mission figs, citrus fruits, persimmons, kumquats, and apples, and local Ojai purveyors provide the freshest of ingredients for the Inn's ever-changing seasonal menus. And each of the seasons is embraced and represented with flavors and flair that are uniquely its own for your palette to savor and enjoy.

Culinary Destinations

THE SEASONAL BOUNTIES OF OJAI ARE
SERVED UP EACH DAY IN DIFFERENT WAYS
AT THE INN'S VARIOUS RESTAURANTS.

MARAVILLA

Sophisticated yet uncomplicated is the signature of
the dishes served at the Inn's fine dining restaurant.
The cuisine highlights garden-grown local and
regional ingredients, prime steaks, chops, and
fresh seafood. The warm décor of the room, the
star-scattered sky from the veranda, its impressive
wine list, and the welcoming, personable service
all create an evening to remember.

JIMMY'S PUB

After a golf game, stop for a sip and a bite at the
Inn's dining "19th hole." Named for Jimmy Demaret,
the Inn's most famous touring golf pro and Master's
Champion, the pub serves original cocktails and
spirits, California microbrewed beers and Central
Coast wines. Its casual bar fare features fresh
salads, sandwiches, burgers, brick-oven pizzas,
and tacos for lunch and dinner.

OAK GRILL

The property's regal 200-year-old oak is front and
center when you gaze at it and the stunning
mountain panorama from the popular vine-covered
pergola on the terrace of the Oak Grill. Whether
dining inside or out, this relaxed setting offers
meals featuring the freshest of ingredients. Their

homemade granola with fresh berries and yogurt or famed eggs Benedict make a delicious breakfast; salads with seasonal vegetables from the Chef's Garden are highlighted at lunch with signature soups, salads, and sandwiches; and dinner favorites include grilled meats and fish, burgers, and pastas.

CAFÉ VERDE

Healthy and refreshing, a spa breakfast or lunch replenishes your taste buds and your senses. At breakfast time, enjoy the fresh juice bar that offers sensational smoothies and fresh roasted coffee. Salads and wraps filled with garden-grown vegetables and organic grilled selections are light and enticing midday meals.

JOE 'N GO

Grab a strong cup of java, some homemade granola, fresh fruit, or a breakfast muffin to go before you hit the golf course. Or, take a quick lunch break with a sandwich and chips before heading out again to play the back nine holes.

HERB GARDEN BISTRO

This Californian bistro situated at the pool and surrounded by the garden's blooming citrus trees, flowers, herbs, and vegetables offers small bites and big bites from crudités, cheese, olives, and almonds to salads and sandwiches.

Spring

The Celebration of Pixie Season

PIXIES—TINY TANGERINES FROM THE MANDARIN FAMILY—PACK A PUNCH OF SWEET, JUICY FLAVOR WHICH THE INN CELEBRATES EVERY YEAR FROM MARCH TO JUNE. KNOWN AS THE BACKYARD FRUIT OF OJAI, THE MICROCLIMATE OF THE AREA PROVIDES ORCHARD GROWERS WITH OPTIMUM CONDITIONS FOR THESE CITRUS DELIGHTS TO THRIVE. THERE ARE ALSO PIXIE TREES IN THE PROPERTY'S HERB GARDEN.

Pixie perfection is highlighted around the resort in numerous ways. Guests' rooms are freshly stocked with mini crates of them for visitors to enjoy, and orange, pixie-shaped soaps are in the bathrooms. Spa treatments are "pixie enhanced," enticing cocktail creations are on hand, and sublime springtime appetizers to desserts are offered.

Learn all about these tasty treats by visiting the Inn's supplier Friend's Ranch, just ten minutes away from the resort. The Friend family and its descendants have been growing fruit in Ojai since the 1880s, are five generations strong, and are a part of the Ojai Pixie Growers Association. Stroll through their historic orchard, visit the packing house, and pick a bag of fresh citrus to take home.

PIXIE COOLER
CAFÉ VERDE

A springtime quencher with or without the rum.

1 Pixie tangerine, peeled
4 fresh mint leaves
1 teaspoon agave nectar

$1^1/_2$ ounces Bacardi
Light Rum
Club soda

In a shaker, muddle the Pixie tangerine, mint leaves and agave nectar. Add the rum and shake. Pour over ice in a tall 12-ounce glass. Top off with club soda and garnish with skewered Pixie segments.

PIXIE COCKTAIL
MARAVILLA

A splendid springtime sipper highlighting Ojai's Pixie orange wonder.

$1^1/_2$ ounces Stoli vodka
$1/_2$ ounce Patron Citronge

$1/_2$ ounce agave nectar
1 slice Pixie tangerine

Combine all ingredients in a cocktail shaker. Shake and then strain into a martini glass; garnish with an orange twist.

PIXIE TANGERINES

Tangerines originated in the Moroccan seaport of Tangiers, hence the name, but these miniature Pixie orange wonders came to fame in the mid-sixties when they were released to the public by the University of California Citrus Research Center. Since then, these lumpy, bumpy fruits are 25,000 trees strong with almost 40 growers in the area who have created the Ojai Pixie Growers Association. A springtime sensation from March until early June, they are seedless, easy to peel, and divine on their own or a welcome addition to any beverage, salad, or dessert as you'll notice on the Inn's seasonal menus.

PINK MOMENT MARTINI

Celebrate the magical moment that can only happen at sunset in Ojai and be seen at the Ojai Valley Inn and Spa. Cheers!

1 1/2 ounces Stoli peach vodka
1 ounce orange juice
1 ounce cranberry juice
1 ounce whipped cream

Shake all ingredients with ice in a shaker. Strain into a martini glass. Garnish with a lemon twist.

PINK HORIZON

Toast the beauty of those pink Ojai skies.

3/4 ounce Luxardo marschino liqueur
1 ounce El Tesoro platinum tequila
1/2 ounce Campari
1 ounce grapefruit juice

Shake all ingredients with ice in a shaker. Strain into a martini glass and garnish with a raspberry, strawberry, blueberry and blackberry skewer.

PINK CHAMPAGNE COCKTAIL

A festive fizzy and rosy celebratory drink using Ojai Valley Inn's Pink Champagne!

1/2 ounce Luxardo cherry liqueur
1/2 ounce Disaronno amaretto
Ojai Valley Inn Pink Moment Champagne

Shake liqueur and amaretto with ice in a shaker. Strain into a chilled Champagne flute. Top off with Ojai Valley Inn Pink Moment Champagne.

PINK MOMENT SMOOTHIE

Think healthy; think pink!

1 ripe banana
1 cup sliced strawberries

Blend the banana and strawberries together with ice in a blender. Pour into a 16-ounce glass. Garnish with a strawberry half.

"I believe in pink."—Audrey Hepburn

"The tones of pink will prevail." —Christian Dior

DELICIOUSLY PINK

The Inn embraces the famous and magical Pink Moment that occurs in the Valley at sunset with delectable "pretty in pink" drinks and cocktails. Like a brilliant setting sky, the shades—from light and rosy to a reddish hue—and the tastes—from juicy to sweet to creamy—of these various pink concoctions vary. Audrey Hepburn, Christian Dior, and Evelyn Lauder all embraced the fashionable glory of the color, and you can, too, with a sip and a toast to that glorious Pink Moment Ojai memory.

ROASTED BABY BEET & PIXIE SALAD
MARAVILLA

*This beautiful salad is a popular seasonal signature item at the Inn, especially
in spring during the Pixie season. The natural sweetness of the beets is brought out even
more by roasting them. The pairing of the tart lavender goat cheese and rich, salty
crushed cashews all come together to make this salad a winner.*

SERVES 2

5 baby beets
Extra-virgin olive oil
Kosher salt to taste
1/8 French baguette, chilled
1 Ojai Pixie tangerine, peeled and
cut into segments
Baby or micro basil or arugula
Splash of white balsamic vinegar

Sea salt and cracked black pepper
to taste
1 teaspoon minced chives
3 ounces Cypress Grove Purple
Haze Goat's Cheese
3 tablespoons dry roasted and
finely chopped cashews

FOR THE BEETS

Rinse the beets under cold water. Toss with a splash of olive oil, season with kosher salt and
wrap up in aluminum foil. Roast in a preheated 375-degree oven until tender. Using a dry
towel you can simply "wipe" off the tops and skin and discard.

FOR THE CROUTONS

Chilling the baguette will help to slice it as thinly as possible. Make 10 slices. Drizzle with
olive oil and press between 2 baking pans. Bake in a preheated 375-degree oven until crisp,
approximately 5 minutes, and then cool.

FOR THE SALAD

In a stainless steel mixing bowl combine the roasted beets, Pixie segments and micro
greens. Add a little of the olive oil and a splash of the white balsamic vinegar and toss.
Adjust the seasoning with sea salt and pepper and add the chives. Spread the goat cheese
on serving plates. Arrange the remaining ingredients as creatively as you like and enjoy!

TRADITIONAL OJAI EGGS BENEDICT

OAK GRILL

This is a decadent and delectable brunch dish that can be enjoyed on a leisurely morning with a glass of fresh orange juice and a cup of strong coffee.

SERVES 2

HOLLANDAISE SAUCE

3 egg yolks	6 to 8 ounces very soft
1 tablespoon water	unsalted butter
1 tablespoon (or more) freshly	Kosher salt to taste
squeezed lemon juice	Dash of cayenne pepper

POACHED EGGS

2 tablespoons distilled white	4 large cage-free 100%
vinegar per 2 quarts water	organic eggs

EGGS BENEDICT

2 English muffins or	4 thin slices Canadian bacon
crumpets, split	1 tablespoon butter

FOR THE HOLLANDAISE SAUCE

Whisk the egg yolks, water and 1 tablespoon lemon juice in a saucepan for 30 seconds or until thick.

Set the pan over moderately low heat and continue to whisk at reasonable speed, reaching all over the bottom and inside of the pan, where the eggs tend to overcook. To moderate the heat, frequently move the pan off the burner for a few seconds, and then back on. As they cook, the eggs will become frothy and increase in volume, and then thicken. When you can see the pan bottom through the streaks of the whisk and the eggs are thick and smooth, remove from the heat.

Add the soft butter in small amounts, whisking constantly to incorporate each addition. As the emulsion forms, you may add the butter in slightly larger amounts, whisking until fully absorbed. Continue incorporating butter until the sauce has thickened to the desired consistency.

Season lightly with kosher salt and cayenne pepper, whisking in well. Taste and adjust the seasoning, adding additional lemon juice if needed. Serve lukewarm.

TO POACH THE EGGS

Fill a saucepan with water to a depth of 2 inches or so. Add the vinegar and bring to a slow boil.

Rapidly crack and open each egg into the water, holding the shell as close to the surface as possible. The eggs will cool the water; adjust the heat to maintain a slow simmer. After a few moments, when the whites have just begun to set, drag the back of a slotted spoon gently across the top of the eggs, to move them off the pan bottom so they don't stick. Cook the eggs for about 4 minutes, adjusting the heat as necessary.

Remove an egg from the water and press both white and yolk. The whites should feel fully set but not too firm and the yolks should feel very soft. Poach longer for firmer eggs.

Remove the eggs from the saucepan with the slotted spoon or strainer and immerse them in a bowl of warm tap water to wash off the vinegar. Set the spoon on a paper towel to remove excess water, and serve eggs immediately.

TO ASSEMBLE THE EGGS BENEDICT

Just before serving, toast the muffins lightly. Warm the ham in a frying pan with the butter.

Center a muffin half on each warm serving plate, cover with a slice of ham and then top with a poached egg. Spoon 1/4 cup hollandaise sauce over each egg; garnish with chopped chives. Serve immediately.

GRILLED CHICKEN WRAP

CAFÉ VERDE & HERB GARDEN BISTRO

This wrap is as healthy as it is tasty because of the delicious combination of fresh ingredients with the roasted garlic aioli. No wonder it is the top selling most asked for lunch time item in the resort!

SERVES 1 OR 2

Roasted Garlic Aïoli (below)
2 (100% whole wheat) lavash flatbread
1 chicken breast, grilled, cooled and shredded
2 cups arugula
1 ripe tomato, cored and julienned

1/2 bulb fennel, shaved as thin as possible
Lemon-infused extra-virgin olive oil
2 tablespoons grated Parmesan cheese
Coarse salt and pepper

Spread Roasted Garlic Aïoli on one side of each sheet of lavash. In a stainless steel mixing bowl combine the shredded chicken, arugula, tomato and fennel. Drizzle with the olive oil. Sprinkle with the Parmesan cheese and season with coarse salt and pepper. Spoon the chicken mixture onto each lavash sheet and simply roll it up. You may refrigerate for up to 3 hours and then slice into serving sized portions. You may substitute your favorite seafood for the chicken or omit the chicken.

ROASTED GARLIC AÏOLI

YIELDS ABOUT 2 CUPS

1 whole garlic head
Olive oil
2 cups premium prepared or homemade mayonnaise

Sherry vinegar to taste
Sea salt to taste

Cut the head of garlic across its equator then drizzle with olive oil and wrap in aluminum foil. Bake in a preheated 375-degree oven for 20 to 30 minutes. Open the foil and bake for another 5 minutes. Using a dry towel, squeeze the hot roasted garlic cloves from the husk. Smash them in a bowl and fold in the mayonnaise. Season to taste with sherry vinegar and sea salt.

OJAI CITRUS AND RASPBERRY TART

This California connection to citrus creates a pretty dessert tart!
SERVES 4 TO 6

OJAI CITRUS CURD

1/2 cup Pixie or regular
tangerine juice
Zest of 2 Pixie or regular
tangerines

2 eggs
2 egg yolks
1/2 cup sugar

ASSEMBLY

1 (9-inch) pie shell, or
4 (4-inch) tart shells
Raspberry jam
Sweetened whipped cream

Fresh raspberries
Pixie tangerine zest
(optional)

FOR THE CURD

Combine all ingredients in a heatproof bowl and whisk to combine. Place the bowl above a pot of simmering water, creating a *bain marie*. Whisk until the curd has thickened to a ribbon stage; remove from the *bain marie*.

TO ASSEMBLE

Prebake the pie shell or tart shells and allow to cool completely before assembling. Spread some raspberry jam on the bottom of the pie shell. Fill with the Ojai Citrus Curd. Refrigerate for at least 4 hours.

Remove from the refrigerator and top with sweetened whipped cream and fresh raspberries. Top with Pixie tangerine zest.

ALL GREEN SMOOTHIE
CAFÉ VERDE

All green, all delicious, all good for you!

2 handfuls of spinach
1/2 cucumber, peeled and seeded
2 sprigs of parsley
5 or 6 celery stalks
1 green apple, peeled, quartered and seeded

Process all ingredients in a juicer. Serve at room temperature or over ice.

ORGANICALLY OJAI

Ojai, with its unique location near clear blue skies, sparkling blue waters, brilliant sunshine, and magnificent mountains, mirrors the weather and topography of the Mediterranean. Hence, the magic of the European basin can be pleasingly replicated here and provides an incredible bounty of produce that results in the best-of-the-best local organic and sustainable ingredients. Besides growing fresh fruits and vegetables on the property, the Inn's culinary team are fully committed to creating memorable meals by working with local purveyors, growers, farmers, and ranchers. Family-owned Ojai businesses such as New Oak Ranch, Friend's Ranch, Rio Gozo, and Watkins Cattle Company are all important partners who work with the Inn to complement your visit and experience.

HERB GARDEN

The Inn embraces the beauty of the natural elements of the Ojai Valley in many ways, but nature is at its finest in the Herb Garden. It is perhaps the most pronounced and peaceful part of the property with its Tea Houses perfect for a picnic, a quiet moment, or meditation (or even a marriage proposal!); its picturesque pool; and its pastoral setting with Valley views (also ideal for a wedding!). Fruit trees—from apple to fig, pear to persimmon, lemon, orange, and Pixie—line pathways. Lush bushes of rosemary and thyme are abundant, and the fragrances of lavender and citrus fill the air.

The Chef's Garden within the premises also highlights the various varieties of organic seasonal vegetables being grown and harvested. There is everything from four varietals of heirloom tomatoes in summer to acorn squash in fall; kale, onions, and beets in spring and Belgian endive and carrots in winter.

The Herb Garden is the perfect place for your own personal escape, where you can relax, reflect, rejuvenate, and "find your moment".

Summer

The Celebration of Lavender Season

THE BRILLIANT BLAZE OF PURPLE AND ITS ENCHANTING AROMA GREETS YOU UPON YOUR SUMMERTIME ARRIVAL AT THE INN. OJAI'S MEDITERRANEAN CLIMATE PROVIDES OPTIMUM CULTIVATING CONDITIONS FOR THE SEVEN LAVENDER VARIETALS GROWN THROUGHOUT THE RESORT GROUNDS. YOU'LL FIND THE OILS THAT CARRY CALMING AND HEALING QUALITIES IN THE AROMATHERAPY TREATMENTS AT THE SPA, ITS SWEET FLAVOR IN CERTAIN CULINARY CREATIONS, AND ITS PRETTY FLOWERS ON DISPLAY IN THE ROOMS.

Annually, lavender is celebrated in town the last weekend of June at the Ojai Valley Lavender Festival where its many uses and tastes are highlighted and promoted. And a visit to nearby New Oak Ranch guarantees a fun and memorable experience where you can picnic and pick your own fresh bunch. Learn how the herb is grown and harvested, turned into therapeutic oils or infused into homemade jams, sugars, and salts that are all available to take home as a fond remembrance of Ojai.

THE NEFF

This year-round drink is named in honor of Wallace Neff,
the original architect who designed the Clubhouse in 1923.
The Wallace Neff Historical Rooms at the Inn
highlight all that he created.

1 ounce St. Germain liqueur
3/4 ounce blackberry brandy
1 ounce lemonade
Juice of 1/2 lime
2 blackberries
Sprig of lavender

Combine the liqueur, brandy, lemonade and lime juice with ice in a shaker;
shake to mix well. Strain into a chilled martini glass. Garnish with a skewer
of 2 blackberries and a sprig of lavender.

LOVELY LAVENDER

Lavender, with its provocative shade and evocative sweet scent, has been loved and
embraced for centuries. It is from the Latin word *lavo*, meaning "to wash" that the herb
took its name and how it came to be used for healing and cleansing. But lavender is also a
prominent ingredient in cooking. England's Queen Victoria loved the floral flavor in her tea
and insisted it be used to "spice" up her scones. Growing wildly in Provence, the French use
it as a meat tenderizer and in their famous honey. Acres of lavender grow here in Ojai from
mid-June to early August. The Inn's culinary creations of lavender in drinks and desserts will
leave you wanting more!

SPA-TINI

CAFÉ VERDE

Clear, cool and refreshing!

1 cucumber
$1/2$ ounce tonic water
$1^1/2$ ounces sake
$1^1/2$ ounces Cruzan vanilla rum

In a shaker, muddle 1 (1-inch) piece of chopped peeled cucumber in tonic water. Add the sake and rum. Shake vigorously. Strain into a chilled martini glass. Garnish with thin slice of cucumber floating on top.

LAVENDER VARIETALS

The Inn pays homage to Ojai's summer season of lavender by planting seven different varietals around the resort. Below are the names of each type and where on the property they can be found.

English Lavender: Herb Garden
French Lavender: Paseo Villas, Fontana
    Building, Villa Los Padres, Spa Ojai,
    Casa Blanca, Villa Mariposa, Artist
    Cottage, Casa Loma
Goodwin Creek Lavender: Main Pool,
    Casa Blanca, Villa Mariposa, Spa Ojai

Grosso Lavender: Spa Ojai, Main Pool
Provence Lavender: Herb Garden,
    Main Pool
Spanish Lavender: Herb Garden, Spa Ojai
Sweet Lavender: Fontana Building

TOPA TOPA MOUNTAIN GRANOLA
CAFÉ VERDE & JOE 'N GO

*Breakfast in Ojai is hearty and healthy, and the added California
zip here is orange juice. This is a great on-the-go snack when
on an early morning hike or a delightful start to the day when mixed
with natural yogurt and fresh berries.*
SERVES 4

1 cup quick-cooking oats
1 tablespoon bran
1 tablespoon pumpkin
   seeds
1 tablespoon crushed
   walnuts
1 tablespoon chopped
   pecans
1 tablespoon sliced almonds
2 tablespoons shredded
   coconut

2 tablespoons maple syrup
1 cup orange juice
1 tablespoon melted butter
2 tablespoons chopped
   dried apricots
2 tablespoons chopped
   dried cherries
2 tablespoons raisins
1 teaspoon natural vanilla
   extract
1 tablespoon brown sugar

In a preheated 275-degree oven, toast the oats, bran, pumpkin seeds, walnuts, pecans, almonds and coconut separately and let cool. In a small saucepan combine maple syrup, orange juice, melted butter and vanilla and bring to a boil. Combine with the oats, bran, nuts and coconut in a large bowl and mix well. Spread the granola on a sheet pan and bake at 275 degrees until it becomes golden in color. Let cool for 20 minutes. In a steel bowl combine the cooled granola with the dried fruit and brown sugar.

Heirloom Tomato Salad
Maravilla

*While enjoying the property in the months of June through early
September, it's difficult not to spot the Inn's famous heirloom tomato garden.
Every summer, the Chef's Garden produces well over a thousand
pounds of four varieties of delicious heirloom tomatoes. These tomatoes are
then handpicked by the culinary team and used exclusively
in recipes like this one.*
Serves 4

Torn Croutons
Day-old foccacia or olive bread
2 tablespoons extra-virgin olive oil
Coarse sea salt to taste

Green Goddess Dressing

All-natural Caesar salad dressing	1 bunch tarragon
	Salt to taste
1 avocado	2 teaspoons lemon juice
1 bunch basil	

Tomatoes and Plating

Selection of 3 different Heirloom tomatoes,	Cracked black pepper to taste
1 tomato of each variety	2 cups Burrata mozzarella cheese
Sherry vinegar to taste	
Coarse sea salt to taste	

For the Croutons
Using your fingers, pinch and pull small pieces of bread from the loaf and
toss them in a mixing bowl with the olive oil. Lay them out flat on a sheet
pan and bake in a preheated 300-degree oven until dry and crunchy. Season
with coarse salt.

For the Dressing
Pour the dressing into your food processor or blender. Add the avocado and
fresh herbs and blend until smooth. Adjust the seasoning with salt and lemon

juice and store in the refrigerator. (At the Inn the Caesar Salad Dressing is made from organic free range eggs and used as the base for the dressing. Making a Caesar dressing from scratch can be a bit ambitious for any home cook so choose a premium, all-natural prepared dressing as the base.)

FOR THE TOMATOES AND PLATING

Just prior to serving use a sharp knife to cut each variety of tomato into a different shape; there are no rules here, just use your creativity and have fun. In a stainless steel mixing bowl, toss the tomatoes with a small splash of sherry vinegar and season them with coarse salt and pepper. Spread a generous amount of the dressing on serving plates. Place some of the tomatoes as you like on top of that, and spoon the cheese between the tomato slices. Top with croutons. Garnish with a sprinkle of coarse sea salt and a drizzle of extra-virgin olive oil and enjoy.

HEIRLOOM TOMATOES

The tantalizing tomato has come a long way from its 1519 arrival into Spain courtsey of explorer Ferdinand Cortez, who brought the seeds back from South America. A fabulously nutritious fruit, versatile vegetable, or both, it doesn't matter as it thrives as an heirloom variety. The rich tapestry of colors and the diversity of kinds and shapes are a bonus to the amazing depth of flavor each varietal produces. On the Inn's property, the Chef's Garden grows four different types—*Cherokee Purple*, *Green Zebra*, *Brandywine Yellow*, and *Mr. Stripey*—that when ripe are hand picked and show up as signature dishes on the menus highlighting these summertime splendors.

JIMMY'S CRAB ROLL
JIMMY'S PUB

This lunchtime favorite from Jimmy's Pub is a refreshing and simple way to use Dungeness crab meat. Served chilled, this mixture can be made a day in advance and kept refrigerated until ready to serve. We use a toasted pretzel bread roll, but the sandwich would be equally delicious on sliced bread or even whole wheat hot dog buns.
SERVES 4

CRAB MEAT
Meat from 1 fresh Dungeness crab
1/2 cup minced red onion
1/2 cup minced celery
1/2 cup minced red bell pepper
1 tablespoon minced flat-leaf parsley
2 tablespoons mayonnaise
Old Bay Seasoning to taste
Kosher salt to taste
Cracked black pepper to taste
Lemon juice to taste

Using your fingers, pick through the crab meat carefully to remove any shell pieces that may still be intact. In a large stainless steel mixing bowl, combine the crab meat, onion, celery, bell pepper, parsley and mayonnaise and mix well. Season to your personal taste with Old Bay Seasoning, kosher salt, pepper and lemon juice.

SANDWICHES
Butter
4 hoagie-style pretzel bread buns, split
1 head romaine, shredded
1 cup Thousand Island dressing

Heat a nonstick pan to medium high. Spread a small amount of butter on the buns and toast until golden. Place your desired amount of crab meat on the bun. Top generously with the shredded lettuce and Thousand Island dressing.

FIGGY FREE-RANGE CHICKEN AND GARDEN THYME MIXED SUMMER GRILL

OAK GRILL DINNER

Summers in Ojai are a time to relax by the one of the Inn's pools and enjoy simple meals from the grill. This is the perfect dish to complement those longer, low-key days and evenings. Most guests like eating later in the day after enjoying the Pink Moment sunset and when the temperatures have dropped. This is a popular choice. The versatile Balsamic Fig Jam is a mouthwatering marinade that also works well on Berkshire Pork, Hook & Line Pacific Salmon, and even tofu!

SERVES 4

1 cup grapeseed oil

4 cage-free organic chicken breasts, skin-on

8 sprigs of fresh thyme

8 cloves of garlic, peeled and smashed

Juice of 1/2 Ojai lemon

Kosher salt and ground pepper to taste

1 cup Balsamic Fig Jam (page 123)

Balsamic vinegar to taste

1 organic green zucchini, cut lengthwise into 1/4-inch slices

1 organic yellow squash, cut lengthwise into 1/4-inch slices

1 organic red onion, cut into 1/4-inch slices

The day prior to cooking, combine 1/2 cup of the grapeseed oil, the chicken, 1/2 the fresh thyme and 1/2 the garlic in a stainless steel mixing bowl; cover and refrigerate.

Preheat your grill to medium-high. Remove the thyme sprigs and any garlic pieces from the marinade. Squeeze the lemon juice over the chicken, then pat dry with paper towels and season both sides with kosher salt and pepper.

Make sure your grill is clean from debris and give it a light spritz of nonstick pan spray to ensure there is no sticking. Place the chicken skin-side down and cook for 5 minutes, watching for flare-ups. Turn once and continue cooking for 5 minutes. At this point the chicken will be very close to being done. Remove the chicken from the direct heat and glaze or baste with the Balsamic Fig Jam. This is applied at the end of the cooking process to avoid burning. Glaze as much as you like!

In a stainless steel bowl, combine the remaining grapeseed oil, a splash of balsamic vinegar, the zucchini, squash, onion and the remaining garlic. Toss until well coated; season with salt and pepper. Grill for 1 to 2 minutes on each side; remove from grill.

Now that your chickens are cooked and the veggies are grilled, crumble the remaining fresh thyme over everything and enjoy!

These flavors pair well with tart goat cheese and lavender—both Ojai favorites. Leftovers could be chopped and combined to make a delicious pasta.

BALSAMIC FIG JAM

OAK GRILL OR
HERB GARDEN BISTRO

There are several big Mission fig trees growing in Ojai and on the Inn's property. This fruit is used in a number of dishes. Use fresh figs or dried Mission figs that are available year-round. The Inn pairs the versatile Balsamic Fig Jam with California cheeses on its Charcuterie platter, and chefs use it to baste meats such as their Figgy Free-Range Chicken.

4 cups dried Mission figs, stems removed
2 cups all-natural honey
4 cups filtered water
2 tablespoons balsamic vinegar, or to taste
Coarse sea salt to taste

In a large, heavy-bottomed pot combine the figs, honey and water. Simmer over low heat until the figs fall apart and the liquid is reduced by one-third. Purée in food processer; add the balsamic vinegar and season with salt to your personal taste. Purée until well combined. Cool and store in the refrigerator.

FIG TREES

The oldest fruit in the world, often described as weird and wonderful, the fantastic fig originated in Asia Minor and now grows throughout the Mediterranean, especially in Sicily and Greece. Thought to have grown in the Garden of Eden where Adam recovered his dignity with a fig leaf in front of Eve, it grows well in Ojai, too. You will see fig trees planted in the Inn's beautiful Herb Garden and around the property. Popular in sweet or savory dishes, terrific fresh or preserved, seasonal fig specialties are on the menu from June to October.

LAVENDER HONEY CRÈME BRÛLÉE

MARAVILLA

These flavors and quintessential elements are Ojai at its sweetest!
This simple brûlée is a hit with guests and locals alike, and it will be a luscious
finale to any at-home dinner party, especially when
served with Citrus Shortbread Cookies.

SERVES 4

1 cup heavy cream	1/4 cup sugar
1/3 cup milk	1 tablespoon honey
1 teaspoon dried lavender	Raw sugar, as needed
5 egg yolks	

Combine the cream and milk in a stainless steel saucepan and bring to a boil; remove from the heat. Add the dried lavender and cover with plastic wrap. Allow to infuse for 10 minutes, or until the desired lavender flavor is reached.

In a separate bowl, combine the egg yolks, 1/4 cup sugar and honey. Whisk until mixed. Strain the lavender milk into the egg yolk mixture, discarding the lavender leaves. Whisk until fully incorporated.

Divide the lavender custard among 4 (6-ounce) ramekins and set inside a large casserole dish. Place the casserole dish in the center of the oven. Fill the casserole dish with hot water without getting any into the ramekins. Bake in a preheated 325-degree oven for 20 to 30 minutes or until the crème brûlée is set.

Remove the casserole dish from the oven, being careful not to get any water into the ramekins. (If there is water in the ramekins, you can remove the water by placing a corner of a paper towel to absorb the water.) Let cool for 10 minutes on the counter before removing from the casserole dish. Refrigerate at least for 4 hours.

Sprinkle with raw sugar. Use a kitchen torch to caramelize the top, using a circular motion. If a kitchen torch is not available, set your oven to broil, and place the crème brûlées on a cookie sheet and position on the top rack with the door open. Check often and rotate to have an even caramelized top.

Decorate with fresh berries and serve. Serve with Citrus Shortbread Cookies.

CITRUS SHORTBREAD COOKIES
MARAVILLA

Ojai is never in short supply of citrus, particularly lemons and oranges!
Gently zest the outer exterior of the fruit to give these delicious shortbread cookies a
hint of citrus flavor. These are paired with the Inn's Lavender Honey Crème Brûlée,
but they are also delicious on their own for a summertime treat.

MAKES 1 DOZEN COOKIES

1 stick butter, softened
3/4 cup sugar, plus more
for sprinkling
1 teaspoon orange zest

1 teaspoon lemon zest
2 1/4 cups all-purpose flour plus
additional for dusting

Cream the butter, sugar, orange zest and lemon zest in a bowl using the paddle attachment of electric mixer for about 5 minutes or until light and fluffy. Add 2 1/4 cups flour and mix until incorporated. Wrap in plastic wrap and refrigerate at least 4 hours. Remove from the refrigerator. Roll out until 1/4 inch thick on a surface dusted with additional flour. Cut into your desired shapes and place on a parchment-lined cookie sheet. Bake for 4 minutes, then turn the cookie sheet halfway around. Bake for 4 minutes longer or just until golden brown. Remove from the oven and immediately sprinkle additional sugar on top. Allow to cool.

For a special treat, scoop your favorite all-natural vanilla bean ice cream between two cookies to make ice cream sandwiches.

Autumn

The Celebration of the Harvest Season

OJAI'S MIGHTY OAKS ACKNOWLEDGE AUTUMN WHEN THEIR LEAVES TURN TO HUES OF RUSTIC REDS, BRIGHT ORANGES, AND YELLOWS, GIVING THE GROUNDS OF THE RESORT A COMPLETELY DIFFERENT COLORFUL LOOK WHEN YOU HIKE, WALK, OR PLAY GOLF AMIDST THE TOPA TOPA MOUNTAINS. NUMEROUS FIREPLACES CRACKLE AND GLOW, WHETHER IN-ROOM, AT THE SPA, OR IN THE VARIOUS DINING VENUES WHERE YOU CAN RELAX AND ENJOY THE UNIQUE ELEMENTS OF OJAI'S AUTUMN.

California bounties abound, and the region harvests olives, apples, pears, pomegranates, persimmons, and kumquats. The Inn's menus deliciously reflect that with cocktails and seasonal fall dishes.

Thanksgiving is celebrated here in a big, happy way with horse-drawn carriage rides through the property on the Wednesday before. On the day itself, guests indulge in the Inn's annual Thanksgiving Grand Buffet, featuring all of the traditional fixings with a California twist.

Ojai Apple Crush Cocktail
Maravilla

A perfect fall fruit concoction served at the Inn during autumn.

1 fresh apple, peeled and chopped
Nutmeg to taste
Allspice to taste
Cinnamon to taste
2¹/₂ ounces Maker's Mark
1 ounce maple syrup
2 ounces apple cider or apple juice

Muddle the apple, nutmeg, allspice and cinnamon in a shaker. Add the Maker's Mark, maple syrup and cider and fill with ice. Shake to mix, then strain into a martini glass and garnish with an apple slice and a cinnamon stick.

APPLES

The apple has an allure all its own. Eve coaxed Adam with it, William Tell shot an arrow through it, one a day will keep the doctor away, and a student is happy to give a teacher one. The pilgrims planted the first United States apple trees in Massachusetts, but now different varietals—from red, green, and yellow—grow in abundance in California. Ojai, with its deep-set valleys where cold air can pool, is an ideal location for apples to thrive. Apple trees are located on the property, and the Inn acknowledges the autumn harvest with small crates of apples in your room for a snack as well as with different dishes and drinks on their fall menus.

HOLE-IN-ONE

SPICED PUMPKIN PIE MARTINI

HOLE-IN-ONE
JIMMY'S PUB

*Celebrate that hole-in-one with this rich
and indulgent cocktail.*

1½ ounces Van Gogh espresso vodka
1 ounce Bailey's Irish cream liqueur
1 ounce Godiva white chocolate liqueur
½ ounce Fernet Branca
Old Rasputin Stout

Combine the first 4 ingredients in a Collins glass.
Top off with Old Rasputin Stout.

THE SCRATCH PLAYER
JIMMY'S PUB

This drink will do any golfer proud!

Chili powder
Salt
1½ ounces Kettle One Citron
½ ounce chili-infused olive juice
Bloody Mary mix, seasoned tomato juice,
or V-8 cocktail juice
Dash of Tabasco sauce

Dip the dampened rim of a pint glass in a mixture
of chili powder and salt. Combine the vodka and
olive juice in the prepared glass. Top off with
Bloody Mary mix. Sprinkle with Tabasco sauce.
Garnish with a celery slice and skewer with an
olive, a slice of lime and a cooked jumbo shrimp.

TEE'D OFF
JIMMY'S PUB

*Enjoy this refreshing beverage when you
are teeing down after a great round of golf or
relaxing on a summer day.*

2 ounces Jeremiah Weed sweet tea vodka
½ ounce Limoncello
3 ounces lemonade

Combine all the ingredients with ice in a shaker.
Shake and serve over ice in a tumbler.

SPICED PUMPKIN PIE MARTINI
JIMMY'S PUB

A festive holiday drink that is a dessert unto itself.

1½ ounces Cruzan vanilla rum
1 ounce spiced pumpkin liqueur
1 ounce Godiva white chocolate liqueur

Combine all the ingredients with ice in a shaker;
shake to mix. Strain into a martini glass and garnish
with a dollop of whipped ceam and a sprinkle of
cinnamon.

Harvest Charcuterie Platter

SPICY OLIVE AND HERB GARDEN THYME TRIO

HERB GARDEN BISTRO

With our abundance of different types of olive trees throughout the valley, this easy snack or party starter speaks to the hills surrounding the Inn. It is terrific served with the Charcuterie platter, too.

1 cup niçoise olives, drained
1 cup Picholine olives, drained
1 cup kalamata olives, drained
1 tablespoon crushed red chili flakes
Pinch of cayenne powder
3 cups extra-virgin olive oil
Freshly picked thyme to taste
Pinch of kosher salt

Combine the olives in a ceramic bowl. Combine the chili flakes, cayenne pepper and olive oil in a small saucepan. Simmer over very low heat for 20 minutes. Pour over the trio of olives and let cool. Sprinkle with freshly picked thyme and enjoy. Make these olives memorable by baking them with soft goat's cheese and serving with a crusty baguette!

OLIVES AND OLIVE OIL

Athena, the Greek Goddess of wisdom, was wise enough to realize the diversity of the almighty olive when she gifted it to the Greeks as an emblem of peace and prosperity. Since then, many warm weather countries in the Mediterranean such as Spain, Italy, Greece, Portugal, and Southern France all grow and export various types of olives and olive oil around the world. Stateside, the shimmering olive is perfectly happy to call Ojai its California home, where groves of these majestic trees grace the hillsides and are harvested from November to January. The Inn highlights different kinds of olives on its menus, places bottles of local Ojai olive oil on the table and uses both in the preparation of its cuisine.

KUMQUAT GINGER COMPOTE
OAK GRILL BREAKFAST OR ON THE CHARCUTERIE PLATTER

Kumquat trees are nestled throughout the grounds of the Inn
but are most prominently displayed on the beautiful Oak Grill patio. The
season for these funny winter fruits generally runs from November
through March. We like to eat them whole right off the vine, but their sweet
juicy rind and somewhat sour fruit makes for complex cooked
flavors. Here's a favorite recipe that's as versatile as it is easy to make. It goes
great on everything and is a nice complement to the Charcuterie.

4 cups whole kumquats
3 tablespoons grapeseed oil
1 tablespoon minced shallot
1 tablespoon minced fresh ginger
Pinch of crushed red chili flakes
Coarse sea salt to taste
1 tablespoon rice wine vinegar, or to taste

Slice the kumquats and remove the seeds as you go. In a heavy-bottomed sauté pan, heat the grapeseed oil to medium. Add the shallot, ginger and chili flakes and sauté lightly for just a few moments until translucent. Add the sliced kumquats and toss to coat. Season with the sea salt, then cover and place into a preheated 375-degree oven. Bake for 30 minutes, stirring occasionally. Remove from the oven and add the rice wine vinegar to your personal taste. Store in an airtight container in the refrigerator.

CHARCUTERIE 101

Assemble a charcuterie platter with whatever you like best. It is an easy and diversely delicious hors d'oeuvre tray or ideal as a first course shared among guests. Typical offerings are cheeses, olives, dried and cured meats, crisp raw vegetables, and fresh fruit alongside compotes, crusty bread, and crackers. The name comes from French "charcutiers," fifteenth century food tradesmen and butchers, who found ways to preserve pork through salting and air-drying. Charcuterie platters have come a long way and are now on menus and at tables worldwide, including at the Inn!

BUTTERNUT SQUASH AND FRANGELICO BISQUE

MARAVILLA

Butternut squash is at its peak in early fall. This luscious soup has a sweet, nutty flavor that is naturally accentuated with the hazelnut flavor of the Frangelico. Arborio rice is used in risotto and will give the soup a velvety texture when puréed.

SERVES 4

1 butternut squash	2 tablespoons arborio rice
Canola oil	4 cups low-sodium vegetable stock
Kosher salt to taste	1 cup Frangelico (hazelnut liqueur)
1 tablespoon grapeseed oil	Apple cider vinegar to taste
4 shallots, sliced	2 tablespoons butter
4 cloves of garlic, crushed	

FOR THE SQUASH

Cut the whole butternut squash vertically in half. Scrape out and discard the seeds using a metal spoon. Rub canola oil on the cut sides and season with kosher salt. Place the squash cut side down on a rimmed baking sheet and add 1/2 cup water to prevent burning. Bake in a preheated 375-degree oven until tender. Turn the squash over and allow to brown for another 10 minutes.

FOR THE SOUP

Scoop the squash out of the skin and reserve. Discard the skins. In a large heavy-bottomed saucepan, heat the grapeseed oil to medium. Add the shallots, garlic and rice and sauté until tender. Add the squash; season lightly with kosher salt. Sauté over lower heat for 5 minutes. Add the stock. Simmer over low heat for 1 hour, stirring occasionally.

In a separate pan, cook the Frangelico over medium heat for 5 minutes or until the alcohol is cooked off. Purée the soup mixture in a blender or food processor until very smooth; return to the heat. Adjust the seasoning to your personal taste with a little apple cider vinegar, salt and the reduced Frangelico. Finish by stirring in the butter or omit to create a delicious vegan soup.

ONE-BITE TRUFFLED GRILLED CHEESE SANDWICHES

A mainstay in the Inn's catering and banquet department, these delicious one-bite mini sandwiches make the perfect sophisticated comfort nibble for your next cocktail party.

MAKES **12** PIECES

1 loaf unsliced brioche bread   4 tablespoons (about) butter
4 slices fontina cheese   1 tablespoon all-natural honey
Italian truffle oil to taste   Kosher salt to taste

Freeze the loaf of bread for 2 hours prior to slicing. [Freezing it will allow you make very thin (1/4-inch) slices easily.] Lay 4 slices flat and top each with 1 slice of cheese. Drizzle with the truffle oil and top with 4 slices of bread. Heat a nonstick pan over medium-high heat and add a small piece of butter. When the butter begins to foam, swirl the pan and add your sandwich. Brown on both sides and repeat until all sandwiches are toasted, adding butter as needed. Trim the crusts and cut each sandwich into three equal-sized portions. Drizzle each with a little of the honey and sprinkle with the kosher salt. Present as you like and serve.

CARAMEL APPLE PIE

Apples grow in abundance in Ojai and are a prominent fruit for fall.
This pie honors the season well and is also served as a Thanksgiving dessert at the Inn.

PIE CRUST

3 cups all-purpose flour	1 stick butter, chilled
1 teaspoon salt	1/3 cup ice water
1 teaspon sugar	1 tablespoon white vinegar
1/2 cup plus 1 tablespoon shortening, chilled	1 egg, beaten

FILLING

6 cups sliced peeled Granny Smith apples	1/4 cup all-purpose flour
2 tablespoons lemon juice	1 teaspoon vanilla extract
1/2 cup packed light brown sugar	1 teaspoon cinnamon
1/2 cup sugar	1/4 teaspoon nutmeg
1/2 stick butter	1/4 teaspoon salt
1/4 cup heavy cream	1/8 teaspoon ground cloves

STREUSEL TOPPING

1 stick butter	1 cup all-purpose flour
1/2 cup sugar	2 teaspoons cinnamon

FOR THE PIE CRUST

Chill all ingredients and your food processor. Combine the flour, salt and sugar in a food processor. Cut in the shortening and butter until the mixture resembles cornmeal.

In a separate bowl, mix the ice water, vinegar and beaten egg. Add the liquid mixture to the flour mixture 1 tablespoon at a time to form a soft dough. Wrap in plastic wrap and refrigerate for at least 4 hours.

Roll out into an 11-inch circle 1/4-inch thick. Spray a 9-inch ovenproof pie plate with nonstick cooking spray and gently lay the prepared pie dough in so that the pastry is pushed in completely. Trim off any excess pie dough from the sides and decorate the edge as desired. Place in the refrigerator until needed.

FOR THE FILLING
Sprinkle the apples with lemon juice. In a large, heavy-duty stainless steel saucepan, combine both sugars and the butter. Cook over medium heat for 5 minutes until a nice caramel color, stirring constantly so the sugar will not burn. Add the cream and stir. Toss in the apple slices, reduce the heat to low and continue to cook the apples for about 8 minutes until softened. Turn off heat.

Combine the dry ingredients in large bowl. Toss to mix. Add to the apple mixture and mix thoroughly. Spoon into the pie shell.

FOR THE STREUSEL TOPPING
Cream together the butter and sugar until light and fluffy, about 5 minutes. In a separate bowl, combine the flour and cinnamon. Add to the butter and sugar and mix just until incorporated to the size of peas. Sprinkle over the pie. Bake in a preheated 375-degree oven for 15 minutes. Reduce heat to 350 degrees and bake for 45 minutes longer.

Winter

The Celebration of the Serenity Season

WINTER IS HOLIDAY TIME, WHERE FANTASTIC DECORATIONS AND THE WARMTH OF LIGHT FROM HANUKKAH MENORAHS AND CHRISTMAS TREES SET THE SCENE FOR THE INN'S SERENITY SEASON. THE FESTIVITIES BEGIN WITH THE RESORT'S ANNUAL TREE-LIGHTING EVENING, WHEN THE MELODIC SOUNDS OF THE OJAI YOUTH SYMPHONY SERENADE GUESTS SIPPING HOT COCOA AND MUNCHING ON DELECTABLE TREATS. A GIANT GINGERBREAD HOUSE GRACES THE LOBBY THROUGHOUT THE SEASON, AND SPECIAL FUN-FILLED ACTIVITIES CREATE FOREVER MEMORIES FOR VISITORS.

Mrs. Claus and her elves tell classic Christmas tales on storytelling evenings, the Artist Cottage holds wreath-making classes; there are horse and carriage rides around the property; and holiday drinks and meals abound. The Inn continues the spirit of the season with a sparkling New Year's Eve bash for guests as they say goodbye to one year and hello to the next—all in sophisticated, serene style.

THE MISTLETOE

*Christmas comes but once a year, and this colorful
cocktail is a delicious way to enjoy it! Garnish with maraschino
cherries or fresh cranberries!*

$1^1/2$ ounces sambuca
$1/2$ ounce cranberry juice
1 to 2 teaspoons pineapple juice

Combine all the ingredients with ice in a shaker; shake to mix well. Strain over ice into a Collins glass. Add skewered garnish of choice and a sprig of mint.

CALIFORNIA COCOA

*This yummy, grown-up hot chocolate will warm your
heart and soul on a cold winter's night!*

2 tablespoons chocolate syrup	1 ounce Godiva white chocolate liqueur
1 cup warm milk	Whipped cream
1 ounce amaretto	Shaved chocolate, sprinkles or candy pieces

Stir the chocolate syrup into the warm milk. Stir in the amaretto and chocolate liqueur. Top with a generous dollop of whipped cream and sprinkle with shaved chocolate, sprinkles or candy pieces.

THE MISTLETOE

EGGNOG BRIOCHE FRENCH TOAST

OAK GRILL

This decadent breakfast dish rolls out every December at the Inn and is a holiday recipe tradition. The richness of the eggnog works well with this simple French toast recipe and adds a tasty festive surprise!

SERVES 2 TO 3

3 cage-free organic eggs
2 cups eggnog
1 teaspoon all-natural vanilla extract
Pinch of kosher salt
Pinch of ground cinnamon
1 teaspoon dark rum
6 thick slices day-old brioche or other artesian bread
1 tablespoon butter

Whisk together the eggs, eggnog, vanilla, kosher salt, cinnamon and rum in a bowl. This can be done a day ahead and stored in the refrigerator.

Dip the bread in the eggnog mixture; let it soak a few seconds. Heat a large sauté pan over medium-low heat and then add half the butter. Pan-fry the sliced bread until golden on both sides, flipping once. Repeat with the remaining egg mixture and bread, adding butter to the pan as needed.

This delicious French toast is great served with fresh berries, bananas and toasted almonds, maple syrup, or Nutella.

LATIN SPOT PRAWN SATAY
MARAVILLA

*Spot Prawns are flavorful and delicious on their own, either simply grilled or sautéed.
You can use other shrimp if you cannot find Spot Prawns. In this preparation, the
rich Spanish history of Ojai is acknowledged with Spanish paprika, chorizo, and limes.
These bamboo skewers can be served as hors d'oeuvres or a main course.*

SERVES 4 AS A MAIN COURSE OR 6 AS AN HORS D'OEUVRES

12 bamboo skewers
12 Spot Prawns, head, body and
shells removed (you can buy
them that way)
2 tablespoons oil
4 ounces Mexican chorizo, cooked
and cooled
3 tablespoons minced shallots
2 tablespoons minced garlic

1 tablespoon smoked Spanish
paprika
2 sweet banana peppers, sliced
1 cup dry white wine
1 tablespoon butter
Kosher salt to taste
Cracked black pepper to taste
Freshly squeezed lime juice
1 small bunch cilantro, minced

Carefully skewer each prawn through the center and reserve. In a large sauté pan, heat the
cooking oil over medium heat. Add the chorizo, shallots and garlic to the pan and cook for
several minutes. Add the paprika, banana peppers and prawns and continue cooking,
stirring with a wooden spoon. Be sure that the prawns are all touching the surface of the
pan so they cook evenly. Add the white wine and reduce. At this point, the prawns should
be cooked; remove and arrange them on a serving plate. Whisk the butter into the chorizo
mixture and adjust the flavor with salt, pepper and lime juice to your personal taste. Finish
with the cilantro and spoon over the prawns.

SLOW-COOKED BRAISED BEEF SHORT RIBS

MARAVILLA AND OAK GRILL

When the days begin growing shorter and Ojai's Topatopa mountaintops become frosted in powdery snow, it's time to break out the slow-cooked, soul warming dishes of winter. A year-round favorite, the Inn's slow-cooked beef short ribs become the center of attention on the menu from November to March. Here is a great, simple recipe that also makes a great holiday meal.

SERVES 4

3 pounds boneless beef short ribs
Kosher salt and ground pepper
to taste
3 tablespoons grapeseed oil
1 white onion, finely chopped
2 carrots, chopped
1 celery root, peeled and
chopped
4 cloves of garlic, peeled
and smashed

1 large ripe tomato, crushed and
seeded
1 (750-milliliter) bottle of Ojai
Vineyard's Syrah
3 sprigs of fresh thyme
Few leaves of fresh rosemary
1 bay leaf
3 cups low-sodium organic
chicken stock

Season the ribs an hour prior to cooking with kosher salt and pepper. Pat them dry with paper towels prior to searing them. In a large, heavy-bottomed skillet, heat the oil. Lightly season the ribs with salt and pepper again. Add them to the skillet and cook over medium-high heat until very well browned and crusty, turning once. Transfer the ribs to a shallow enameled cast-iron casserole.

Add the onion, carrots and celery root to the skillet. Cook over low heat for about 10 minutes or until very soft and lightly browned, stirring occasionally. Add the crushed garlic and tomato and sauté for several minutes. Add the wine and the herbs. Bring to a boil over high heat. Add the chicken stock and bring to a boil. Pour over the ribs.

Cook, covered, in the lower third of a preheated 350-degree oven for 2 hours (this should be at the lowest possible simmer, ideally only a few bubbles here and there). When the meat is tender but not yet totally falling apart, uncover and braise for 45 minutes to 1 hour longer, turning the ribs once, until the sauce is reduced by about half and the meat is very tender.

Transfer the short ribs to a clean, shallow baking dish, discard any vegetables sticking to the ribs. Strain the sauce and pour it over the meat.

This process can be done 1 or 2 days ahead of time and chilled, covered, for about 1 hour before serving. This will only make your short ribs more delicious if allowed to "set" for a day. Simply reheat them in the same pan.

The Short Ribs are fantastic served with cheesy polenta, Buttermilk Mashed Potatoes (page 150), root vegetables or tossed with your favorite pasta.

MARAVILLA FILET WITH CABERNET SAUCE

MARAVILLA

A California classic served with potato croquettes and fresh asparagus.
SERVES 2

CABERNET SAUCE

1 tablespoon clarified butter or olive oil	3 sprigs of fresh thyme
4 garlic cloves, smashed	1 small sprig of fresh rosemary
5 shallots, finely diced	1 cup beef stock
2 tablespoons flour	Butter to taste
2 cups cabernet sauvignon	Salt and pepper to taste

Heat the clarified butter in a large stockpot. Heat on medium until hot. Add the garlic and shallots and stir until lightly golden brown. Add the flour and stir for several minutes until the flour turns golden. Add the red wine and herbs; mix thoroughly. Cook until the wine is reduced by half. Add the stock; bring to a simmer and skim any film that forms at the top. Allow the stock to cook down until it's reduced by two-thirds. Strain the sauce through a fine mesh colander into another pot before finishing. Using a wire whisk, stir the butter into the sauce. This will thicken it a bit and add more shine. Adjust the seasoning with salt and pepper just before serving. You can adjust the balance of the sauce with a touch of vinegar, citrus or wine if it gets too rich. Keep warm.

CARAMELIZED SHALLOTS

4 cups water	4 whole shallots, peeled
1 cup sugar	1 tablespoon cooking oil
1 cup red wine vinegar	Salt and pepper to taste

Begin by boiling the water, sugar and red wine vinegar in a small pan. Add the shallots and cook for 5 to 10 minutes or until tender. Drain and cool, uncovered, in the refrigerator. In a sauté pan, heat the oil to medium-high. Add the shallots and allow them to brown on all sides; if the pan becomes too hot, add a little bit of water periodically during the process. Season with salt and pepper.

FILETS AND ASSEMBLY

2 (7-ounce) Watkins Cattle
Company grass-fed beef filets
Kosher salt and cracked black
pepper to taste
Cooking oil

Potato Croquettes (page 151)
25 (about) haricots verts
Butter
Fresh steamed asparagus

Season the beef filets with kosher salt and cracked black pepper. Brush lightly with cooking oil and grill to your desired temperature on a hot preheated grill. While the filets are grilling (allow 10 minute for rare and up to 25 minutes for well done) sauté the croquettes as described. Heat the shallots as described above. Now it's time to plate: use your creativity and artistic skills. Serve with fresh asparagus.

BUTTERMILK MASHED POTATOES

*A perfect and popular side dish at the Inn for any meat or poultry;
the use of buttermilk makes a delicious difference.*

SERVES 4

3/4 cup buttermilk
1 tablespoon unsalted butter

1¼ pounds Yukon Gold potatoes,
peeled and cut into large pieces
1½ teaspoons kosher salt

Combine the buttermilk and butter in a saucepan; heat over a low flame until the butter melts; reserve. Cover the potatoes and 1 teaspoon of the salt with cold water in a large saucepan. Bring to a boil over medium-high heat. Reduce the heat to simmer. When the potatoes are tender when pierced with a fork, about 30 minutes, drain them.

Return the potatoes to the pan and set over low heat, uncovered, for about 5 minutes, stirring occasionally, to let the potatoes dry out a little (too much moisture will not allow them to absorb as much buttermilk). Pass the potatoes through a ricer or food mill. Fold the warm buttermilk mixture into the potatoes a little at a time with a wooden spoon until thoroughly incorporated. Season to taste with the remaining salt and enjoy.

POTATO CROQUETTES
MARAVILLA

SERVES 2

2 large Yukon gold potatoes, peeled	2 whole eggs
1 tablespoon butter	All-purpose flour
1 cup grated Gruyère cheese	Panko bread crumbs
Salt and pepper to taste	1 tablespoon clarified butter or cooking oil

Simmer the potatoes in water to cover in a saucepan for 25 minutes or until potatoes are cooked through; drain. Pass through a food mill or ricer. Fold in the butter, then fold in the grated cheese. Season with salt and pepper. Form into 2- to 3-inch diameter "pucks" and refrigerate. Whisk the eggs in a bowl until smooth. Lightly dust the "pucks" with the flour, then coat them quickly in the egg and gently cover them in the bread crumbs; set aside. When ready to serve, heat a nonstick pan to medium heat and add the clarified butter or cooking oil. Add the "pucks" and brown on both sides. Drain on paper towel.

POTATO LATKES

No Hanukkah celebration is complete without these traditional potato pancakes that the Inn serves at the annual Jewish holiday celebration. The citrus give them a nice California twist. They can be enjoyed at other times of the year, too.
MAKES 12 TO 16 LATKES

2 pounds unpeeled red-skin potatoes	1 teaspoon salt
2 medium onions	1 1/2 teaspoons orange or tangerine zest
2 large eggs, slightly beaten	1 teaspoon baking powder
1/2 to 3/4 teaspoon ground black pepper	1/2 cup flour
	Vegetable oil for frying

Grate or shred the potatoes and onions. Squeeze out any extra liquid. Add eggs, salt, pepper, zest, baking powder and flour. Heat vegetable oil in skillet until very hot. Drop mixture by heaping spoonfuls into hot oil in a skillet. Turn once after first side browns. Drain on brown paper or paper towels. Serve with applesauce and/or sour cream for dipping.

CHANTERELLE MUSHROOM AND
HERB BREAD PUDDING STUFFING

*For a refined yet hearty twist, the secret to this stuffing is the use of
brioche or ciabatta bread combined with the earthy flavors of elegant mushrooms
and a fresh herb combination of thyme, sage, and parsley.*
SERVES 4 GENEROUSLY

$2^1/2$ cups chicken stock or
low-sodium chicken broth
1 large cage-free egg
1 large cage-free egg yolk
1 cup diced onion
$1/2$ cup finely diced celery
8 ounces chanterelle or
oyster mushrooms
2 teaspoons minced garlic

2 teaspoons dried thyme
$1/4$ cup chopped flat-leaf parsley
2 tablespoons freshly chopped sage
6 cups cubed brioche or rustic
Italian-style ciabatta bread
Kosher salt to taste
Pinch of cayenne pepper
6 tablespoons unsalted butter

Butter a 6×10-inch oval baking dish with 2 teaspoons butter; line with parchment paper. Cut a piece of foil large enough to cover the dish. Spray the aluminum foil with nonstick spray and set aside until ready.

In a bowl, whisk together the chicken stock, egg and egg yolk; set aside. Melt 1 tablespoon of butter over medium-high heat in a medium pan. Add onion and celery and cook for about 4 minutes or until softened. Increase heat to high and add the mushrooms, stirring to combine. Cook for 2 minutes, stirring occasionally. Stir in the garlic and thyme. Remove from heat and add the fresh herbs. Transfer mushroom mixture to a bowl and add bread cubes, stirring carefully to combine; season with kosher salt and cayenne pepper. Add chicken broth mixture to the stuffing, stirring until well combined. Place stuffing in the prepared baking dish.

Cover with the foil sprayed side down to avoid the stuffing sticking to the foil. Set the baking dish on a baking sheet. Bake in a preheated 400-degree oven for 30 minutes; uncover, and continue baking 10 minutes more. Remove from oven and let stuffing cool for 5 minutes before serving.

SWEET POTATO GRATIN

The Inn serves this on their holiday buffet for Thanksgiving and Christmas,
and you can, too. It is terrific for a crowd.

SERVES 12

6 large Garnet yams, peeled	1 teaspoon kosher salt or to taste
4 red-skin yams	1 teaspoon white pepper or to taste
1 cup packed brown sugar	1 cup clarified butter
2 tablespoons cinnamon	

Carefully slice the yams on a mandolin into rounds using the natural shape of one end of the yam. Once the yams are sliced, combine all the dry ingredients in a mixing bowl.

Melt the clarified butter in a medium saucepan. If you don't have clarified butter, you can easily melt whole butter in a saucepan over medium-low heat and skim off the milk solids that float to the top. After you have skimmed most of the fat solids out you will have an end result of "clear" clarified butter.

Combine the sliced yams in a mixing bowl. Using a 2-ounce ladle, pour some melted clarified butter onto the sliced yams and spread them in a 2-inch-deep baking dish. Lightly sprinkle some of your dry seasoning spices over the single layer of yam. Repeat the layers until you have run out of sliced yams.

Place an identical baking dish over the yams and compress it with some heavy oven-safe weight. Place the baking dishes over a sheet lined with foil to avoid any spillage in your oven and smoke from the residual clarified butter. Bake in preheated 325-degree oven for 45 minutes.

Devil's Food Cake with Dark Chocolate Caramel Mousse

Serves 8

For the Mousse

12 ounces dark chocolate, broken into pieces

1/4 cup salted caramel

2 eggs

2 tablespoons sugar

2 tablespoons water

2 cups cream

Combine the chocolate and salted caramel in the top of a double boiler. Heat over low heat until melted and well combined. Remove from the heat. Whip the eggs in the bowl of a stand mixer using the wire whip attachment on low speed until very light. Combine the sugar and water in a small saucepan; mix until the sugar is dissolved. Cook over medium heat to 240 degrees on a candy thermometer. Drizzle slowly into the eggs, beating constantly. Beat on high until the mixture triples in volume. Add 2 cups of the cream to the same saucepan and bring to a boil. Add to the chocolate mixture, folding together with a rubber spatula until blended. Fold in the egg mixture. Whip the remaining 2 cups cream in a bowl until soft peaks form. Fold into the chocolate mixture. Pour into a serving dish or mold. Chill for at least 6 hours or preferably overnight.

For the Cake

1/2 cup packed light brown sugar

1 cup granulated sugar

4 ounces butter, softened

2 eggs

1 tablespoon vanilla extract

1 3/4 cups all-purpose flour

1/2 cup plus 2 tablespoons baking cocoa

1 1/2 teaspoons baking soda

1/4 teaspoon salt

1 1/3 cups buttermilk

Preheat the oven to 315 degrees for a convection oven or 350 degrees for a conventional oven. Cream the sugars and butter in the bowl of a stand mixer using a paddle attachment until light and fluffy. Add the eggs one at a time, beating each until fully incorporated and scraping the sides of the bowl with a rubber spatula after each addition. Mix in the vanilla on medium speed. Sift the flour, baking cocoa, baking soda and salt together. Add the dry ingredients alternately with the buttermilk 1/3 at a time, beating well and scraping the bowl after each addition. Pour into 2 (9-inch) cake pans sprayed with nonstick baking spray.

Bake for 15 minutes or until the cake springs back when lightly touched. Cool on a wire rack for 15 minutes before turning out onto parchment-lined surface to cool completely.

FOR THE GANACHE

4 ounces quality dark chocolate,   1 tablespoon butter
broken into pieces   1/2 cup heavy cream

Combine the chocolate and butter in a small mixing bowl and set aside. Bring the cream to a simmer in a small saucepan over medium heat. When cream just reaches the simmering point, pour over the chocolate and butter. Let stand for 30 seconds. Fold the mixture together until incorporated. Fold until completely mixed. Spread the mousse between the cake layers. Top with the ganache for a decadent layer cake.

ALWAYS WANTING S'MORE

Every night, the Inn offers the traditional fixings of marshmallows, chocolate, and graham crackers. Guests of all ages can have fun making this classic campfire treat when they roast their marshmallows at the fire pit, then sandwich them between the chocolate and graham crackers to create their own s'more! They're so delicious everyone will be wanting s'more!

A VERY SPECIAL HOUSE

*Thanks to the Crusaders, gingerbread came to Europe in the eleventh century.
Yet, it was the Brothers Grimm and their seventeenth-century fairy tale of* Hansel & Gretel
*with its candy and cookie house in the woods that put the making of
gingerbread houses front and center. In fact, the making of gingerbread figurines
and houses is still an art form for bakers throughout Germany, Hungary,
England, France, Poland, and Scandinavia. Today, at Christmas time around the
world, gingerbread makes its most impressive appearance. An annual
highlight of the Inn's Serenity Season décor, besides its festive lights and greenery,
is the amazing life-size gingerbread house that graces its lobby.*

*Eight members of the Inn's culinary team spend over 84 hours together creating
this beautiful cookie masterpiece. They use 200 pounds of gingerbread dough to "build"
116 (12×12-inch) gingerbread shingles and 95 (4×4-inch) roof tiles. It takes
81 pounds of dark chocolate and 10 pounds of white rolling fondant to construct the
doorway and windows. This* lebkuchenhaeusel *(German for gingerbread house)
is a stunning sight to see!—but not to eat.*

*The quantities to make the dough and icing—like the finished product itself—
are enormous. The fun ingredients follow.*

GINGERBREAD HOUSE

100 pounds flour	3³/₄ gallons honey
20 pounds brown sugar	1¹/₄ gallons water
10 pounds shortening	10 ounces ground ginger
2 pounds plus 8 ounces	10 ounces ground allspice
of baking soda	20 ounces cinnamon
100 eggs	10 ounces ground cloves

ICING
25 pounds powdered sugar
75 egg whites
64 lemons for juice

Index

A Serene Setting

Historic Ojai

Tastes for All Seasons

Symbols of Ojai

THE HAPPY TIMES AND HISTORY OF THE INN ARE
WELL REPRESENTED IN THE EVOLUTION OF ITS
LOGO OVER TIME.

OJAI VALLEY INN & SPA

Edward Libbey, founder of the Ojai Valley Club and Golf Course, created the first logo in 1923. The Little Scotsman in the plaid knickers and striped cap playing golf emphasized his passion for golf, his love of Scotland, and the renowned St. Andrew's Golf Course there.

The current circular logo came to be in 1986. Divided into eight squares, it contains multiple meanings. Many say the emblems look like wagon wheels from the early days of Ojai farming, while others believe the symbols are abstract orange slices

referring to the numerous citrus groves in the region. The white panels represent flags on the greens of the golf course, and the earth tone shades upon them refer to the colors of the fertile lands. The fact that there are eight of them highlights the Chumash Indians' sun-stick with eight directorial rays of the sun and is a nod to their heritage and ties to the Valley.

The design of ninetieth anniversary logo, created especially to celebrate this momentous milestone, blends a look of Indian feathers and the white panel of a flag on the green to create a winning, celebratory look.